Road Atlas SOUTHERN AFRICA

CW00616883

CONTENTS

	BEIRA	BLANTYRE	BLOEMFONTEIN	BULAWAYO	CAPE TOWN	COLESBERG	DURBAN	EAST LONDON	GABORONE	GEORGE	GRAAFF-REINET	GRAHAMSTOWN	HARARE	JOHANNESBURG	KEETMANSHOOP	KIMBERLEY	LADYSMITH	LIVINGSTONE	LUSAKA	MAFIKENG	MAPUTO	MASERU	MBABANE	MESSINA	NELSPRUIT	PIETERMARITZBURG	PIETERSBURG	PORT ELIZABETH	PRETORIA	UMTATA	UPINGTON	WELKOM	WINDHOEK
WINDHOEK	2704	2763	1559	1625	1480	1539	2207	1953	1715	1853	1663	1822	2029	1781	485	1382	1988	1177	1650	1557	2380	1716	2142	2311	2136	2114	2100	1916	1839	2032	985	1659	•
UMTATA	2173	2608	570	1739	1314	517	439	235	1192	880	503	415	1996	869	1547	747	517	2187	2665	1034	1064	616	1003	1392	976	360	1181	545	928	•	1047	718	2032
PRETORIA	1362	1677	456	808	1460	682	636	1040	350	1229	880	1057	1065	58	1354	530	414	1256	1737	294	583	488	372	461	322	557	250	1133	•	928	854	316	1839
PORT ELIZABETH	2718	2810	677	1941	769	451	984	310	1299	335	291	130	2198	1075	1431	743	1062	2389	2687	1141	1609	822	1548	1594	1434	905	1383	•	1133	545	933	830	1916
MBABANE	1734	2005	677	1180	1680	903	562	1238	719	1450	1101	1418	1401	361	1657	833	386	1628	1972	648	223	633	•	797	173	640	504	1548	372	1003	1157	451	2142
MASERU	1850	2290	157	1421	1160	383	590	630	702	913	599	692	1561	438	1283	334	366	1869	2167	544	853	•	633	949	713	511	738	822	488	616	731	249	1716
MAPUTO	1101	1675	900	1061	1903	1123	633	1301	957	1670	1321	1478	1648	519	1895	1071	567	1509	1988	886	•	853	223	725	244	706	605	1609	583	1064	1395	813	2380
MAFIKENG	1592	1917	398	886	1343	672	821	1048	158	1203	854	1065	1305	287	1072	380	597	1314	1793	•	886	544	648	680	635	742	569	1141	294	1034	572	321	1557
LUSAKA	1054	1113	2010	927	3014	2418	2381	2594	1636	2783	2434	2611	489	1611	2135	2084	2359	473	•	1793	1988	2167	1972	1082	1876	2293	1293	2687	1554	2665	2366	1569	1650
KIMBERLEY	1880	2207	177	1338	962	292	811	780	538	762	490	667	1595	380	897	•	587	1786	2084	380	1071	334	833	991	827	732	780	743	530	747	397	294	1382
JOHANNESBURG	1408	1735	398	866	1402	624	578	982	358	1171	822	999	1123	•	1296	472	356	1156	1611	287	599	438	361	519	355	499	308	1075	58	869	796	258	1781
HARARE	565	612	1521	439	2525	1929	1711	2105	1147	2294	1945	2122	•	1123	2595	1595	1661	852	489	1305	1648	1561	1401	593	1387	1804	804	2198	1065	1996	1877	1080	2029
GABORONE	1434	1759	622	708	1501	848	979	1206	•	1361	1012	1223	1147	358	1230	538	755	1156	1636	158	957	702	719	696	672	900	485	1299	350	1192	730	479	1715
EAST LONDON	2408	2716	584	1848	1079	488	674	•	1206	645	395	180	2105	982	1468	780	752	2296	2594	1048	1301	630	1238	1501	1226	595	1290	310	1040	235	968	737	1953
DURBAN	1734	2323	634	1454	1753	860	•	674	979	1319	942	854	1711	578	1708	811	248	1902	2381	821	633	590	562	1107	707	79	886	984	636	439	1208	564	2207
CAPE TOWN	2810	3136	1004	2268	•	778	1753	1079	1501	438	787	899	2525	1402	995	962	1413	2716	3014	1343	1903	1160	1680	1921	1762	1674	1710	769	1460	1314	894	1156	1480
BULAWAYO	726	1051	1264	•	2268	1490	1850	1848	708	2039	1690	1867	439	866	1938	1246	1222	448	927	866	1061	1421	1180	338	1069	1365	549	1941	808	1736	1438	1187	1625
BLOEMFONTEIN	1806	2132	•	1264	1004	226	634	584	622	773	424	601	1521	398	1074	177	410	1712	2010	464	897	157	677	917	757	555	706	677	456	570	574	153	1559

Although the greatest care has been taken in compiling the kilometre table and ensuring that the road distances given conform to the latest information available, no responsibility for errors can be accepted by the publishers, who would welcome any suggested amendments. The kilometres indicate the shortest distance between any two places over tarred roads wherever possible.

To find the distance between any two places in the table read down and across the respective connecting columns.

An example is given above in which the distance between Cape Town and Pretoria is shown as 1460 kilometres

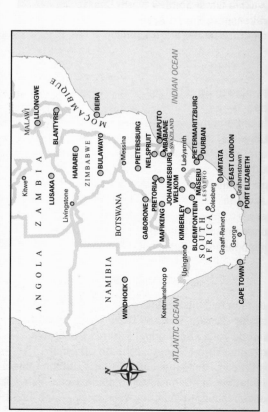

MOÇAMBIQUE'S UNDERWATER WORLD

The seemingly endless string of coral reef that protects the 2500 km coastline of Moçambique is once again becoming a favourite destination for scuba and snorkel divers in Southern Africa. Moçambique is well on the road to recovery since the end of the civil war. After the successful elections in 1994, it is regaining popularity with nature lovers and holiday makers in general. The best diving facilities are to be found on the Paradise Islands (Ilhas do Paraiso) but for the more adventurous there are many excellent diving sites from the Ilha do Moçambique in the north to Ilha da Inhaca near Maputo. The unspoilt coral reefs and shoreline make this area one of the best dive sites in the world.

VICTORIA AND ALFRED WATERFRONT

Linking the modern, bustling city of Cape Town with its historical maritime past, the V&A Waterfront development has in the few years since its inception become the fore-most tourist attraction in South Africa. The rebirth of the "Tavern of the Seas" has attracted local and foreign visitors alike. Surrounding the Victoria Basin, which has been extended to create a marina for yachts and pleasure craft, there are hotels, restaurants, pubs and shops to cater for most tastes. One is able to view, at close quarters, the varied activities of a working harbour which has welcomed such famous ships as the Royal Yacht Britannia, Jacques Cousteau's research vessel and the replica of the Bounty.

ETOSHA NATIONAL PARK

This natural reserve is almost 23 000 square kilometres in area and is home to large numbers of zebra, wildebeest, kudu, springbok, impala, jackal, lion, elephant and giraffe. The numerous waterholes provide tourists with the best opportunities for game viewing. The great pan itself, once a large lake, is now a flat, dry salt pan 130 km long and 70 km wide. The name Etosha means "the big white place" which is an apt description of the shimmering mirage-covered pan. The best months to visit the park are August and September. It is closed in the rainy season - from November to mid March.

VICTORIA FALLS

One of the great natural wonders of the world, these waterfalls on the Zambezi River were named by the Victorian explorer David Livingstone who first saw them from the edge of a 100 metre precipice on an island that lies in the centre of the falls.   The perpetual spray from Mosi-oa-Tunya or the "smoke that thunders" has created a rain forest opposite the falls which forms part of the Victoria Falls National Park, a World Heritage site. A wide variety of bird tand animal life including the sable antelope can be seen in the park. The nearby town of Victoria Falls in Zimbabwe has a number of good hotels, a casino and golf course and tourists are offered launch cruises up the Zambezi, flights over the falls or white water rafting on this "grade 5" river.

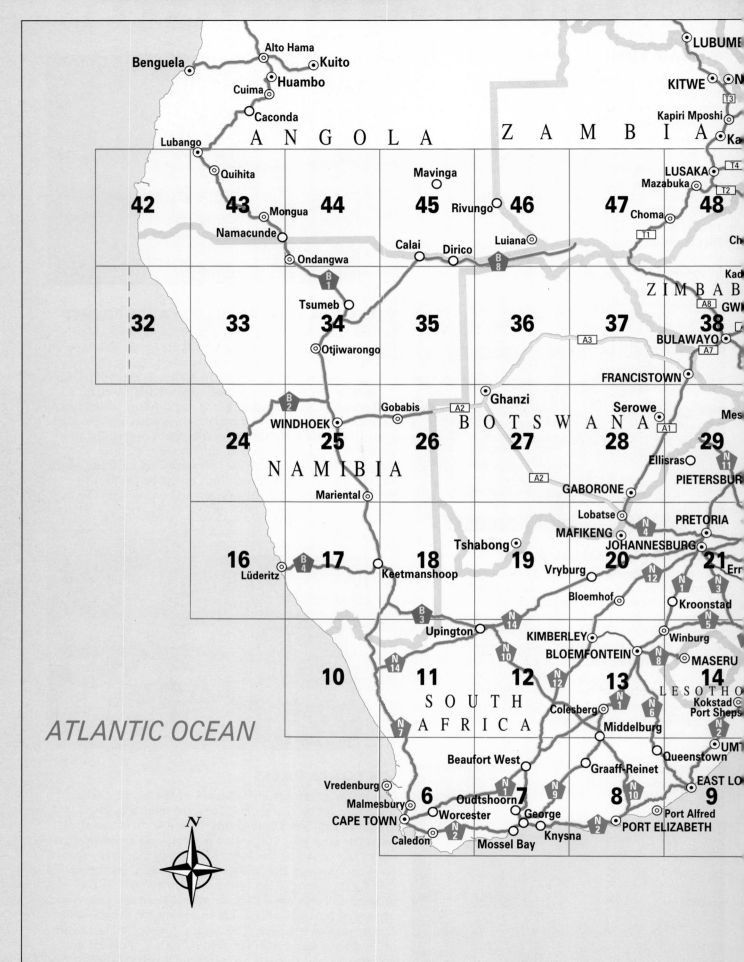

ATLANTIC OCEAN

Copyright ©Map Studio

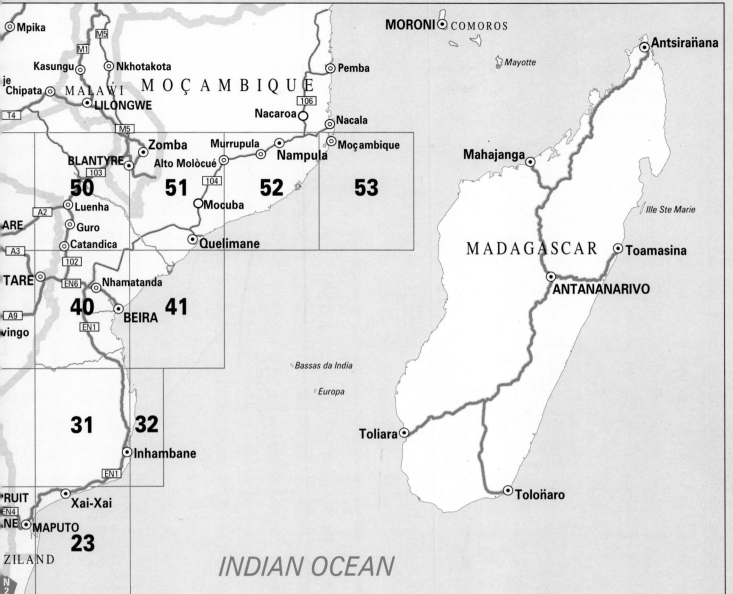

100 200 300 400 500km

Mpika
Kasungu ● Nkhotakota
je
Chipata ● MALAWI
M5
M1
MOÇAMBIQUE
● Pemba
T4
LILONGWE
Zomba Murrupula ● Nacala
BLANTYRE Alto Molòcué Nampula ● Moçambique
Nacaroa
106
50 **51** **52** **53**
104
Luenha Mocuba
A2 Guro
ARE Catandica
A3 Quelimane
102
TARE EN6 Nhamatanda
A9 **40** **41**
EN1 BEIRA

MORONI ● COMOROS
Mayotte
● Antsiranana

Mahajanga ●
Ille Ste Marie

MADAGASCAR ● Toamasina
● ANTANANARIVO

Bassas da India
Europa

31 **32**
● Inhambane
EN1

RUIT Xai-Xai
EN4
NE ● MAPUTO
ZILAND **23**
N2

Toliara ●

● Toloñaro

INDIAN OCEAN

ls Bay

AN

LEGEND TO ATLAS SECTION

0 5 10 20 30 40 50km
Scale 1 : 1 500 000

Reference grid letter / number
Index Grid

tarred under untarred
construction
Freeway and National Road

Principal Trunk Road

Main Road

Secondary Road

Route Numbers

Toll Route and Toll Plaza

15 22 Distances in Kilometres

Mountain Passes

Railway

International &
Provincial Boundary

National Park
and Nature Reserve

Water Features

Capital or City

⊙ Chief Administrative Town

O Major Town

◎ Secondary Town

⊙ Other Town

o Settlement

✈ Major Airport

⊢ Airfield

⌂ Accommodation

• Place of Interest

★ Historical Site

⊿ Border Control

▲ Major Spot Height

Marsh

Waterfall

1 2 3 4
A
B
C
D
E
1 2 3 4

Overlap Area

Page continuation number

Copyright ©Map Studio

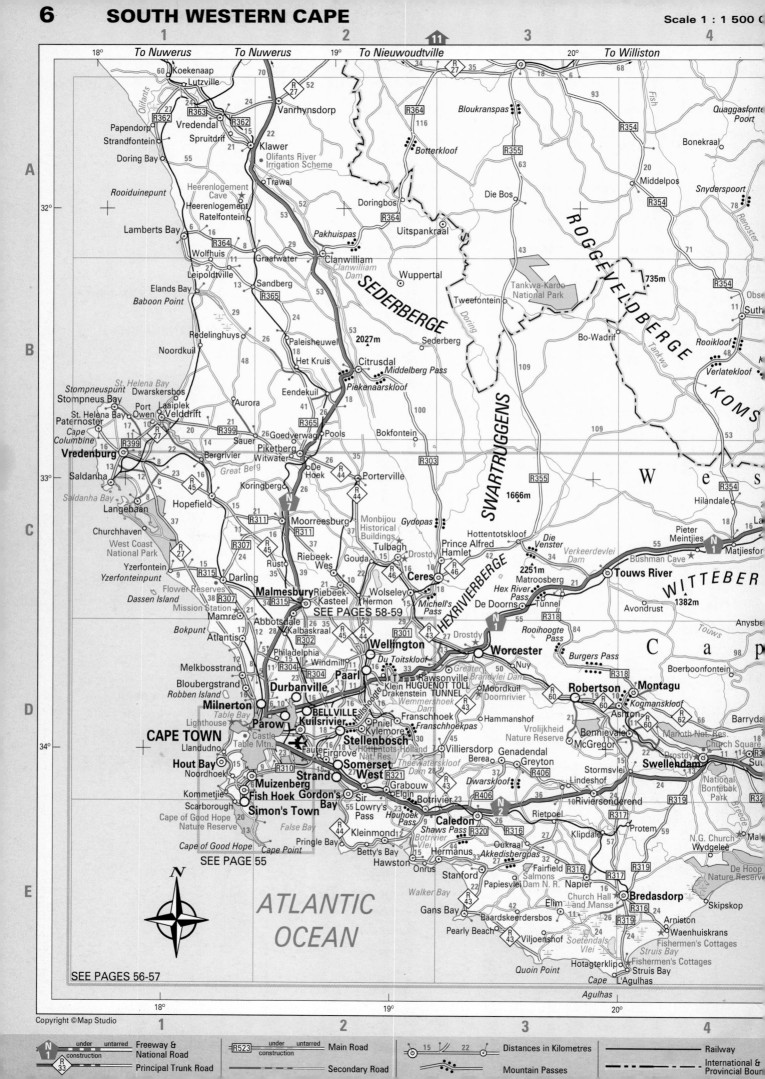

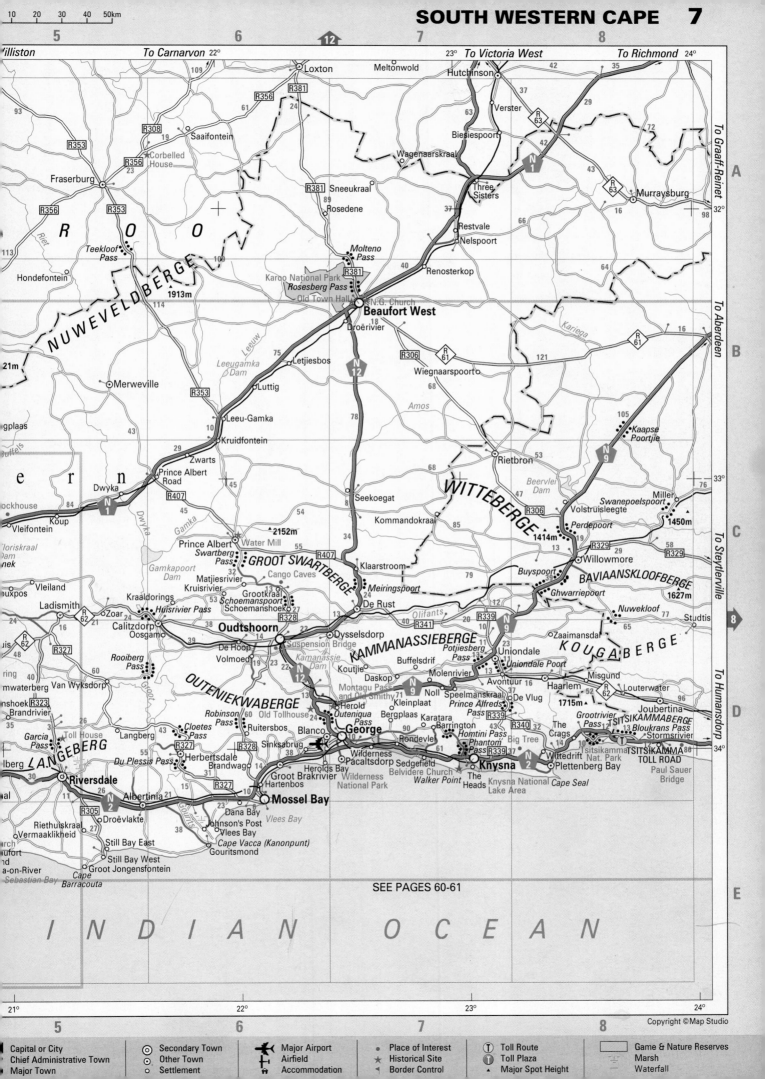

INDIAN OCEAN

Copyright ©Map Studio

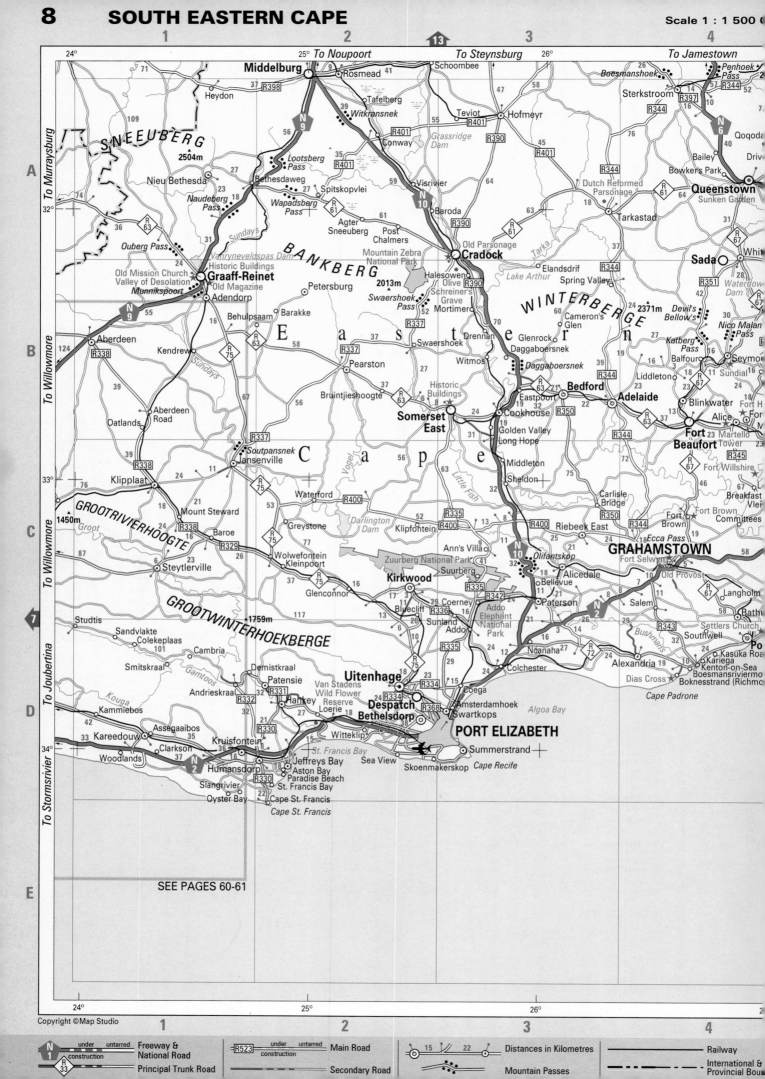

Cape Recife Lighthouse near Port Elizabeth

Copyright ©Map Studio

Legend:

- Capital or City
- Chief Administrative Town
- Major Town
- Secondary Town
- Other Town
- Settlement
- Major Airport
- Airfield
- Accommodation
- Place of Interest
- Historical Site
- Border Control
- Toll Route
- Toll Plaza
- Major Spot Height
- Game & Nature Reserves
- Marsh
- Waterfall

Scale 1 : 1 500 0

SEE PAGE 74

To Grünau

JAKKALSBERGE

Sendelingsdrif

Richtersveld National Park

D316

Khubus

Oranjemund
Alexander Bay
*Border Crossing only
with permit*

Kotzehoop

Noordoewer
Noordoewer

Vioolsdrif

Orange

Haib

Holgat

Eksteenfontein

50

B 1

Lekkersing

29°

74

Anenous Pass

Port Nolloth
Mc Dougall's Bay

93

R382

Steinkopf

N 7

Bulletrap

44

Wedge Point

Nigramoep

R355

Nababeep
Miners' Memorial

Springbok

93

A T L A N T I C   O C E A N

Grootmis
Kleinsee

Buffels

Kommaggas

Melkbospunt

Messelpad Pass

Wildeperdehoek Pass

Soebatsfontein

30°

Skulpfonteinpunt

Koiingnaas

Kamieskr

Hondeklipbaai

Spoegrivier

Kar

Wallekraal

Strandfonteinpunt

Nariep
Groen

Groenriviersm

Island Point

Kotzesr

Flower carpet in Namaqualand

31°

15°

16°

17°

Copyright ©Map Studio

N 1	under construction / untarred — **Freeway & National Road**
R 33	**Principal Trunk Road**
R523	under construction / untarred — **Main Road**
	Secondary Road
15 // 22	**Distances in Kilometres**
	Mountain Passes
	Railway
	International & Provincial Boun

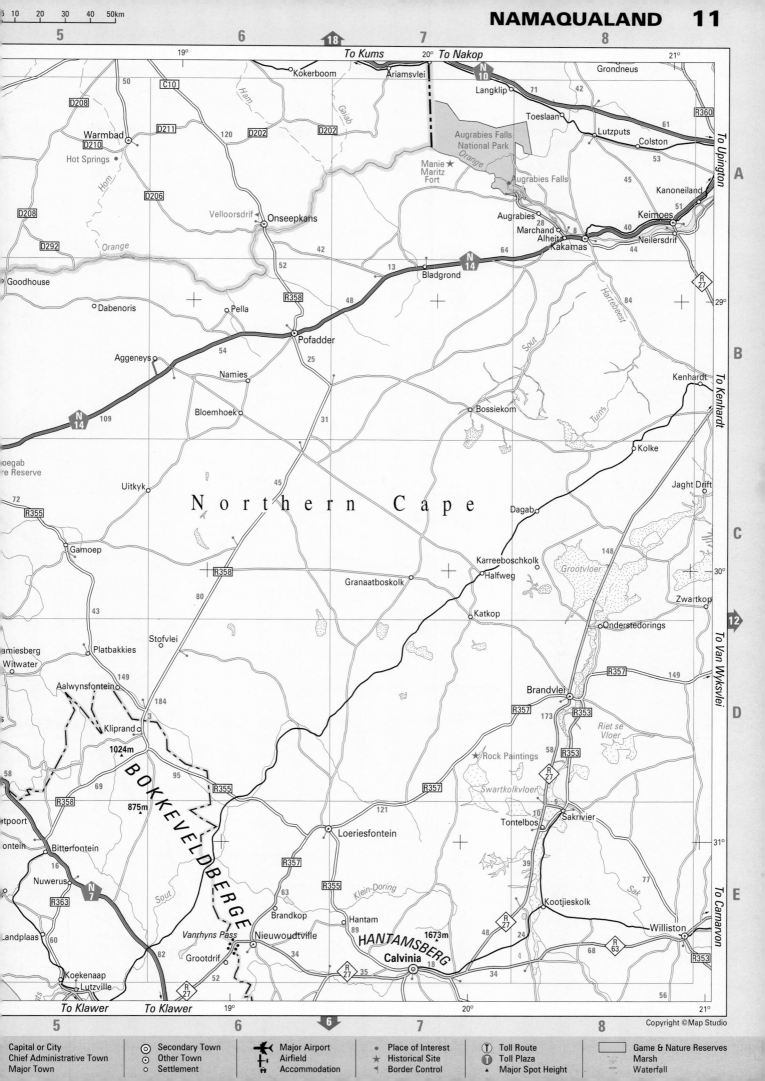

Copyright ©Map Studio

Capital or City	Secondary Town	Major Airport	Place of Interest	Toll Route	Game & Nature Reserves
Chief Administrative Town	Other Town	Airfield	Historical Site	Toll Plaza	Marsh
Major Town	Settlement	Accommodation	Border Control	Major Spot Height	Waterfall

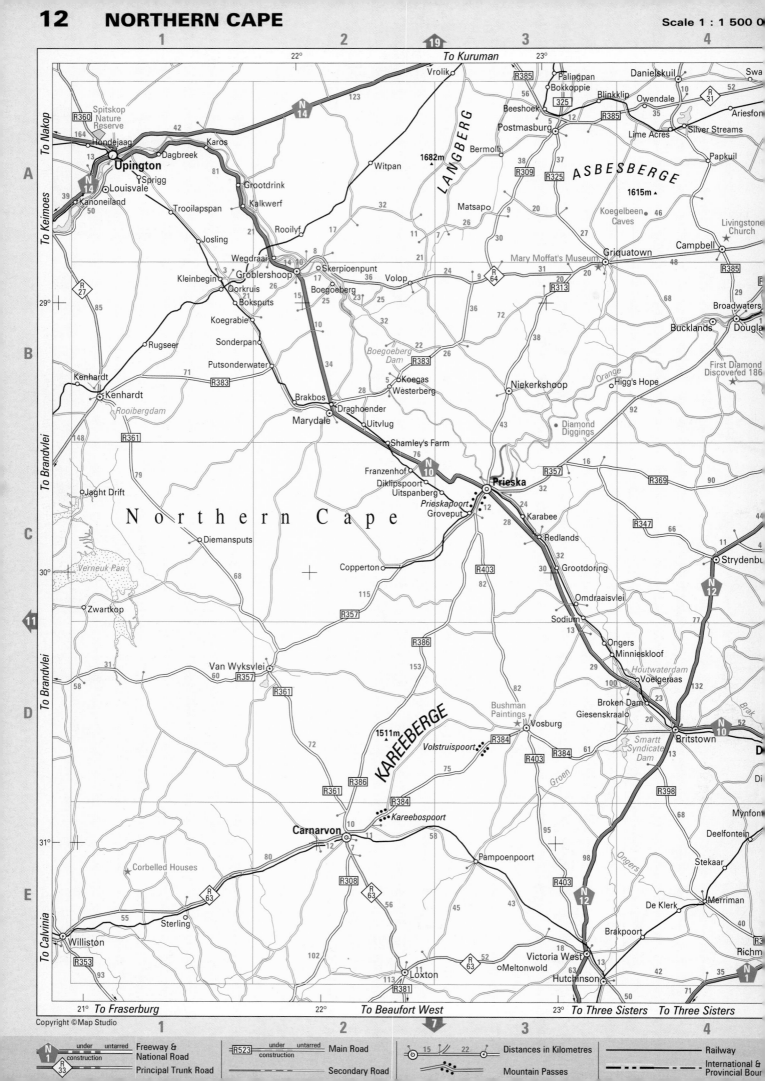

10 20 30 40 50km

To Warrenton 25°   To Wesselsbron   To Virginia 27°

KIMBERLEY

BLOEMFONTEIN

F r e e   S t a t e

Mount Rupert · Hertzogville · Bultfontein · Welgeleë · Theron
Windsorton · Content · R708 · R710 · R30 · R73
Delportshoop · Windsorton Road · R700 · Theunissen
Elandsdrift · R708 · Winburg · Erfenis Dam
Longlands · St. Mary's Anglican Church · Riverton · Boshof · Volkspele Monument · Eensgevonden
Barkly West · Kenilworth · Dealesville · Soutpan · Brandfort · R703
Archaeological Reserve · Spytfontein · Wolwespruit · Florisbad · Spetdoring Nature Reserve · Verkeerdevlei
Big Hole · Carters Ridge 1899 · Modder · Karee · Lumsden's Horse Monument · N1
Koedoesberg · Battle of Magersfontein 1900 · Battle of Poplar Grove 1900 · Battle of Paardeberg 1900 · Glen
Ploeysburg · Ritchie · Modderrivier · Battle of Driefontein 1900 · Raadsaal · Mazelspoort
Glaciated Rocks & Engravings · Petrusburg · De Brug · Woman's Monument · Shannon · Botshabelo · Thaba Nchu
Heuningneskloof · Jacobsdal · Ferreira · Rodenbeck · Sannaspos · Rustfontein Dam Nature Reserve
Graspan · R705 · Oppermans · Koffiefontein · Tierpoort · Meadows
Belmont · Witput · Rooipan · Kalkfontein Dam Nature Reserve · Austin's Post · Dewetsdorp
Wanda · Kalkfonteindam · Riet · Reddersburg · R717 · Jammersdrif
Oranjerivier · Luckhoff · Allep · Edenburg · Caledon Nature Reserve · Wolwepoort · Welbedacht Dam
Orania · Fauresmith · Jagersfontein · Krugers · Gomvlei · Vanstadensrus · Egmont Dam
Kraankuil · R387 · R369 · Vanderkloof · Reebokrand · Trompsburg · Breipaal · Smithfield
Petrusville · Vanderkloof Dam · N.G. Kerk · Lofter · Dupleston · Rouxville
Philippolis Road · Philippolis · Springfontein · Louw Wepener · Koukraal · N6
Philipstown · Waterkloof · Priors · Tussen-die-Rivier Game Farm · Goedemoed
Burgerville · Donkerpoort · Gariep Nature Reserve · Bethulie · Pellissier House and Museum · Hot Sulphur Springs
Hanover Road · Gariep Dam · Oviston · Knapdaar · Aliwal North
Hanover · Dwaal · Norvalspont · Agtergang · Venterstad · Taalmonument · Burgersdorp
Colesberg · Oviston Nat. Res. · Jamestown · Witkop · Vineyard
Noupoort · Carlton · Steynsburg · Stormberg · Molteno · Syfergat · Dordrecht
Sherborne · Middelburg · Rosmead · Schoombee · 2109m · Boesmanshoek · Penhoek Pass · 2127m · STORMBERG · Sterkstroom

To Graaff-Reinet 25°   To Cradock   To Hofmeyr 26°   To Queenstown 27°

To Ventersburg · To Senekal · To Tweespruit · To Hobhouse · To Mafeteng · To Lady Grey

Copyright © Map Studio

Capital or City / Chief Administrative Town / Major Town
Secondary Town / Other Town / Settlement
Major Airport / Airfield / Accommodation
Place of Interest / Historical Site / Border Control
Toll Route / Toll Plaza / Major Spot Height
Game & Nature Reserves / Marsh / Waterfall

To Ventersburg   To Steynsrus   To Arlington   To Warden   To Nev

Libertas
Valsrivier
Kransfontein
Blockhouse
De Beers Pass
Cund
Big

Sand River Convention 1862
Willem Pretorius Game Reserve
Allemanskraal Dam
Bethlehem   Bohlokong
Pretoriuskloof Bird Sanctuary
Aberfeldy
Bushman Raintings
Harrismith
Craigsforth
Driefor

Senekal
Paul Roux
Kestell
Swinburne
Van Reenen Pass
Wyford
Besters
Pepwor

Winburg
Noupoortsnek
Golden Gate Highlands National Park
Sterkfontein Dam
Sterkfontein Dam Nature Reserve
Kerkenberg
Geluksburg
Ladysmith

Voortrekker Monument
Rosendal
2408m
Clarens
2477m
Phuthaditjhaba
Rock Paintings
Oliviershoekpas
Spioenkop Dam N.R.
Roosb
MIDLANDS TOLL ROUTE

Marquard
Fouriesburg
Hendrick's Drift
Monantsa Pass
Libono
Rock Paintings
Bergville
Spioenkop Dam
Battle o

WITTEBERGE
Caledonspoort
Joel's Drift
Sefako
Qhobela
Moteng Pass
Royal Natal National Park
Woodstock Dam
Zunckels
Winterton

Allandale
Ficksburg
Gumtree
Butha-Buthe
Prehistoric Footprints
3282
Cathedral Peak
Frere
Loskop

Excelsior
Clocolan
Khabo
Hlotse (Leribe)
Fort
Maputsoe
Estcourt

Thaba Nchu
Westminster
Peka
Pekabrug
Corn Exchange
Matlameng
3727m
Mothae
Injasuti Hillside
Ntabamhlope

Tweespruit
Ladybrand
Maserubrug
Kolonyama
Koenong
Pitseng
A25
Lejone
Lesotho Highlands Water Scheme
Mapholaneng
Rockmount

Thaba Phatshwa
Kommissiepoort
Mamates
Teyateyaneng
Mapoteng
Nokong
Moletsane
Katse Dam
Seshote
Mokhotlong
Methalaneng
Giant's Castle
Highmoor
Redcliffe
Notti

Glenrock
Leeuwrivierdam
Moshoeshoe's Mountain Fortress
Thaba Bosiu
Bushman's Pass
Bokong
Katse
Kamberg
Loteni
Mkhomazi

MASERU
Mazenod
Roma
Molimo Nthuse Pass
Blue Mountain Pass
Cheche Pass
Mokhoabong Pass
Thaba Tseka
3482m
The Natal Drakensberg Park
Lower Loteni
Mpendle

Hobhouse
Matsieng
Morija
Sehonghong
Boesmansnek
Sani Pass
Himeville Nature Reserve

Caledon
Wepener
Van Rooyenshek
Mafeteng
LESOTHO
Semonkong
3096m
THABA PUTSOA
Sehlabathebe
Sehlabathebe National Park
Bushman's Nek
Himeville
Underberg
Coleford N.R.
Coleford
Bulwe

Rock Paintings
Birdpark
Mopkopung
Patlong
Tsoelike
Ramatseliso's Gate
Kingscote
Donnybrook
Creighton

Boesmanskop
Makhaleng
Sepapushek
Cannibal Caves
Nohana
Qobong
Mokopung
Qacha's Nek
Mafube
Lehlohonolo
Riverside

Makhalengbrug
Ketane
Mohales Hoek
Mt. Moorosi
Mphaki
Roamer's Rest
New Amalfi
Swartberg
Umzimkul
Sneezewood

Zastron
Mekaling
Phamong
Cutting Camp
Sebapala
Tosing
Ongeluksnek
Matatiele
Cedarville
Franklin
Mount Currie N.R.
Bisi

Palmietfontein
Moyeni (Quthing)
Ralebona
Thaba Chitja
Sigoga
Bonny Ridge
Mount Currie N.R.
Stafford's Post

Sterkspruit
Telebrug
Kinirapoort
Colonanek
Kokstad
Weza
Hardin

Bluegums
Herschel
Lundean's Nek
Rock Paintings
Naudesnek
Mount Fletcher
Lahlangubo
Moordenaarsnek
Brooks Nek
Rode
Mount Ayliff
Fort Donald
Bizan

Lady Grey
Karringmelkspruit
2771m
Rhodes
Elands Height
Lower Pitseng
Katkop
Mount Frere
Tabankulu
Magusheni
Ngabeni
Redou

New England
Mosesh's Ford
Halcyon Drift
Tina Bridge
Qumbu
Fort Donald

Clanville
Clifford
Barkly East
Maclear
Ntywenka
Tsitsa Bridge
Flagstaff
Holy Cross
Mkamb
Nature Res

Rossouw
Swempoort
Barkly Pass
Ugie
Qumbu
Stoneyridge
Palmerton
Mkamba

Morristown
Elliot
Ku-Mayima
Tsolo
Sidwadweni
Lusikisiki
Port Grosvenor

Indwe
Cala Road
Ida
Xalanga
Quiba
Garryowen
Calapas
Cala
Whitmore
Ntibane
Umtata Dam
Nobantu
Libode
Mlenganapas
Ntshilini
Gemvale
Embotyi

Eastern Cape

DRAKENSBERG

To Bloemfontein
To Rouxville
To Aliwal North
To Molteno
To Engcobo   To Umtata   To Port St. Johns

Copyright ©Map Studio

under construction / untarred — Freeway & National Road
under construction / untarred — Principal Trunk Road
under construction / untarred — Main Road
Secondary Road
15   22   Distances in Kilometres
Mountain Passes
Railway
International &

10 20 30 40 50km

To Vryheid   31° To Vryheid   To Nongoma   To Mkuze

Dundee
Nondweni
Nhlazatshe
Hlabisa
Bushlands
Cape Vidal

Nqutu
Mahlabatini
Hluhluwe
Umfolozi
Park

Wasbank
Vant's Drift
R68
 Uloliwe
Ilangakazi
Umfolozi
Game
Reserve
N2

Rorke's Drift
Silutshana
Babanango
Ulundi
Nodwengu
Ulundi 1879
Ondini
Mtubatuba
St. Lucia
R618
Riverview

Isandhlwana
Elandskraal
Mangeni
Dingaan's
Kraal
Umunywana
Kwa
Mbonambi
Lake Eteza
Nature Reserve
Teza
Mapelane Nature Reserve

Helpmekaar
Pomeroy
Qudeni
Osborn
Melmoth
Dondotsha
Mposa

KwaZulu - Natal
Tugela Gorge
Nkandla
Randalhurst
Ndundulu
Nkwalini
Enseleni Nature Reserve

SEE PAGES 62-63

Tugela Ferry
Cetshwayo's Grave
Dlolwana
The Ranch
Empangeni
Richards Bay

Keate's Drift
Muden
Ntunjambiti
Entumeni
Bulawayo Site of Shaka's Kraal
Coward's Bush
Monument
Felixton
Richards Bay Game Reserve

Kranskop
Eshowe
Fort Nongqai
Mtunzini
Umlalazi Nature Reserve

Greytown
Ahrens
Battle of
Gingindlovu
Amatikulu

General Louis Botha's Birthplace
KwaSizabantu
Mission
Fort Mtombeni
Mapumulo
Nyoni
Gingindlovu

Rietvlei
Otimati
Mandini
Tugela
NORTH COAST TOLL ROAD
Battle of Tugela 1838

Sevenoaks
Darnall
Tugela Mouth
Fort Pearson

York
Dalton
Fawnleas
Shaka's Memorial
Aldinville
Ultimatum Tree
Zinkwazi Beach

New Hanover
Shakaskraal

Howick
Albert Falls
Nature Reserve
Mpolweni
Albert
Falls
Wartburg
Sheffield Beach
Umhlali
Salt
Rock

Merrivale
Valley of 1000 Hills
Shaka's Rock
Ballito

PIETERMARITZBURG
Colenso Mission
Station 1854
Tongaat
NORTH COAST
TOLL ROAD

Hilton
Ashburton
Verulam
Newsel and
Umdloti Beach

Mpumalanga
Camper-
Kranskloof
Nature Reserve
Inanda
Phoenix
Umhlanga

MARIANNHILL TOLL ROAD
Clermont
KwaMashu

INDIAN OCEAN

Rosebank
Pinetown
DURBAN

Queensburgh
Umlazi
Umbumbulu
The Bluff

Isipingo

Rhodes' House
Adams
Mission
Umbogintwini
Amanzimtoti
Kingsburgh

Dududu
Umgababa

PAGES 64-65
Vernon Crookes
Nature Reserve
Umkomaas
Clansthal

R612
Umzinto
Scottburgh
Park Rynie

Braemar
Kelso
Pennington
Sezela

R102
Ifafa Beach
Mtwalume
Turton

St. Faith's
Dweshulu
Hibberdene
Umzumbe

Marburg
Southport
Sea Park
Umtentweni

Port Shepstone
Shelley Beach

R620
Uvongo
Margate
Ramsgate
Southbroom
Palm Beach
Glenmore Beach

Umtamvuna Nature Reserve
Port Edward

E PAGES 62-63

Copyright ©Map Studio

A view of "The Amphitheatre", Drakensberg

Symbol	Meaning					
Capital or City	Secondary Town	Major Airport	Place of Interest	Toll Route	Game & Nature Reserves	
Chief Administrative Town	Other Town	Airfield	Historical Site	Toll Plaza	Marsh	
Major Town	Settlement	Accommodation	Border Control	Major Spot Height	Waterfall	

Scale 1 : 1 500 0

1   2   24   3   4

13°   14°   15°

25°

A

Franciscus Bay

Oystercliffs o

B

ATLANTIC OCEAN

Mercury Island o
Spencer Bay o

K a r a s

26°

Hottentots Bay   o Hottentot

Ichabo Island ·

C

Lüderitz Bucht

Lüderitz
Diaz Point
Site of original Diaz Cross
Ghost Mining To
Ko

27°

Elizabet
Possession Is

D

Albatros
Pomo

Ghost town of Kolmanskop

E

28°

13°   14°   15

Copyright ©Map Studio

1   2   3   4

N 1	under untarred	Freeway &
R 33	construction	National Road
		Principal Trunk Road

R523	under untarred	Main Road
	construction	
		Secondary Road

15	22	Distances in Kilometres
		Mountain Passes

Railway

International &
Provincial Bou

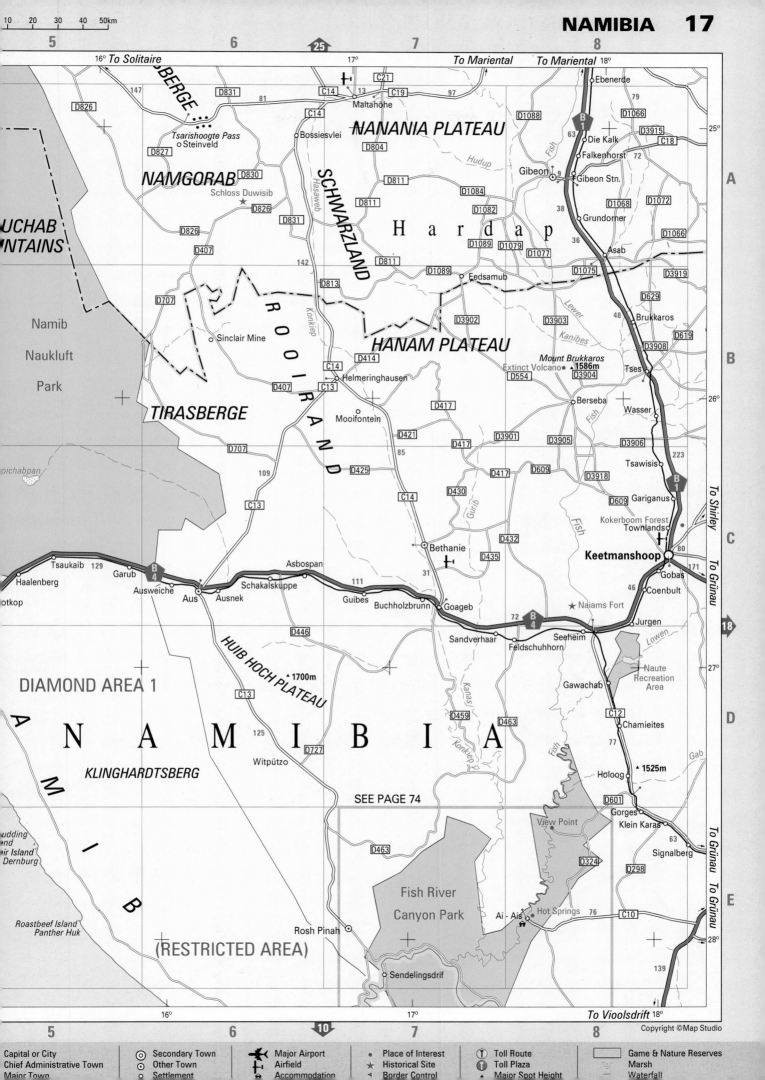

10 20 30 40 50km

5   6   25   7   8

16° To Solitaire   17°   To Mariental   To Mariental 18°

Ebenerde

...BERGE   147   D831   81   C14   C19   97   C21   D1088   79   D1066

D826   C14   Maltahöhe   D19   B1   63   Die Kalk   C18

          Tsarishoogte Pass   Bossiesvlei   NANANIA PLATEAU   Falkenhorst   72

D827   o Steinveld   Hudup   Gibeon   9   Gibeon Stn.   25°

NAMGORAB   D830   D804   D811   Grundorner   D1068   D1072   **A**

          Schloss Duwisib ★   D811   H a r d a p   38   D1066

          D826   D1084   D1082   D1089   Asab   D3919

D826   D831   SCHWARZLAND   D1089   D1079   D1077   36   D1075

D407   D811   Eedsamub   D1075   Lewer   D629

          D813   Kanibes   48   Brukkaros   D619

D707   R   Sinclair Mine   D3902   D3903   D3908   **B**

          O   D414   HANAM PLATEAU   Mount Brukkaros   Tses

          O   C14   Helmeringhausen   Extinct Volcano ● ▲1586m   D554   D3904

          I   D407   C13   Berseba   Wasser

TIRASBERGE   R   Mooifontein   D417   Fish   26°

          A   D421   D417   D3901   D3905   D3906   Tsawisis   223

D707   N   D425   85   D417   D609   D3918   B1

oichabpan   D   109   D430   D609   Gariganus

          C13   C14   D432   Kokerboom Forest

          Bethanie   D435   31   Townlands   80   **C**

Tsaukaib   129   Garub   Asbospan   111   **Keetmanshoop**   171

Haalenberg   B4   Schakalskuppe   Guibes   Buchholzbrunn   Gobas   To Shirley

otkop   Ausweiche   Aus   Ausnek   Goageb   72   B4   Coenbult   46   To Grünau

DIAMOND AREA 1   D446   Sandverhaar   Feldschuhhorn   Seeheim   Jurgen   **18**

          HUIB HOCH PLATEAU   ▲1700m   ★ Naiams Fort   Lowen   27°

N A M I B I A   125   Naute Recreation Area   Gawachab

          C13   KLINGHARDTSBERG   D459   D463   Fish   C12   Chamieites   77   **D**

          D727   Witpützo   Konkiep   Holoog   ▲1525m   Gab

          SEE PAGE 74   D463   D601   Gorges   To Grünau

          Fish River   Klein Karas   63   To Grünau

          D324   D298   Signalberg

          Roastbeef Island   Panther Huk   Rosh Pinah   View Point   Ai-Ais   Hot Springs   76   C10   28°   **E**

          (RESTRICTED AREA)   Sendelingsdrif   139

16°   10   17°   To Vioolsdrift 18°

5   6   10   7   8

Copyright ©Map Studio

Capital or City   ◎ Secondary Town   ✈ Major Airport   ● Place of Interest   Ⓣ Toll Route   Game & Nature Reserves
Chief Administrative Town   ◉ Other Town   Airfield   ★ Historical Site   Ⓣ Toll Plaza   Marsh
Major Town   ○ Settlement   Accommodation   Border Control   Major Spot Height   Waterfall

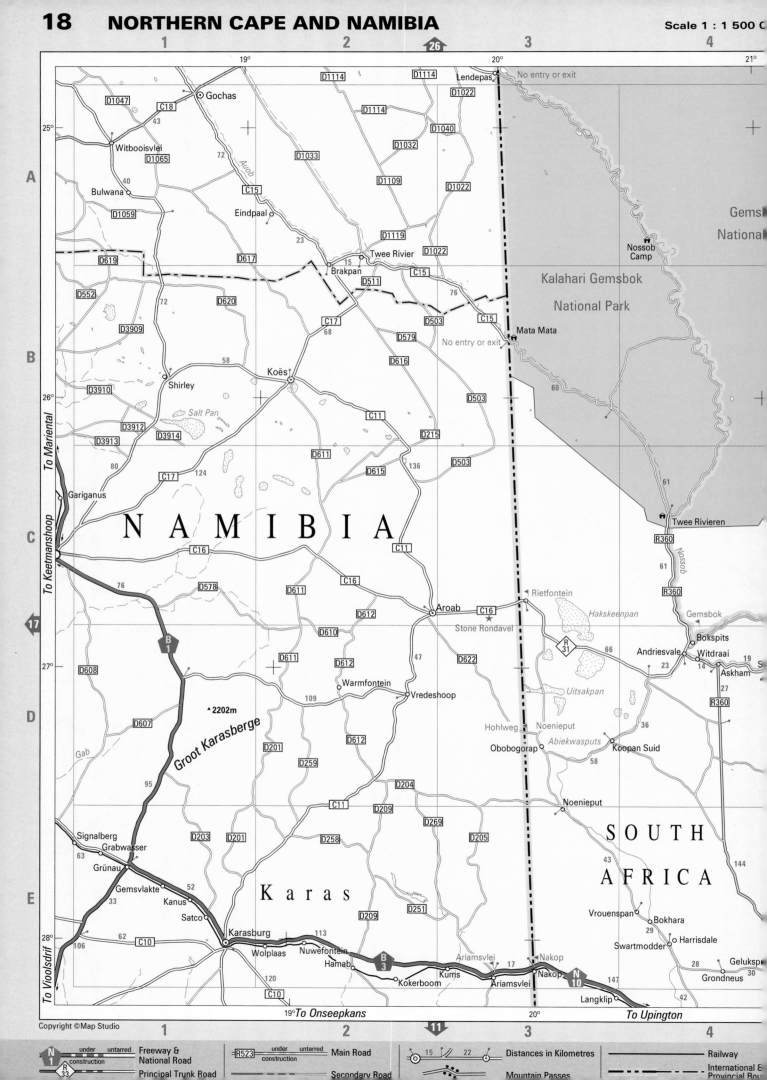

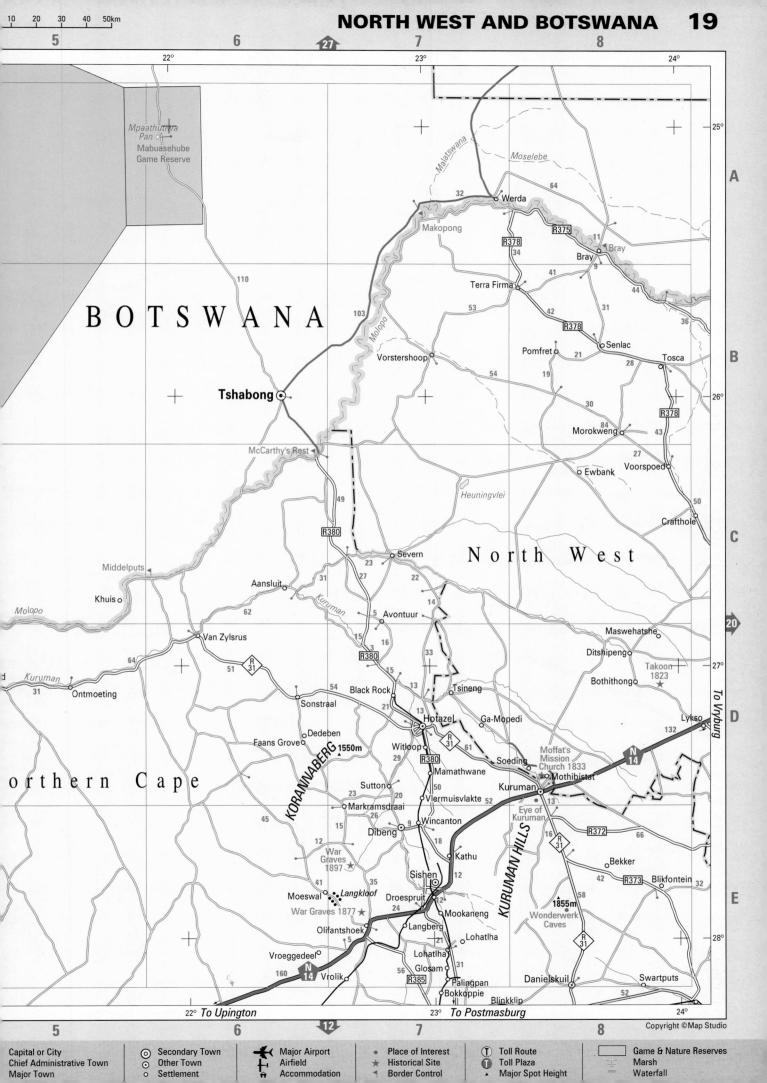

10 20 30 40 50km

5   6   27   7   8

22°   23°   24°

Mpaathutlwa
Pan
Mabuasehube
Game Reserve

110

B O T S W A N A

64

32 Werda
Makopong
Moselebe
Malatswana

R378 R375 11
Bray
34 Bray 9
Terra Firma 41
53 42 R378 31 44
Pomfret 21 Senlac 28 Tosca
103 54 19 R378
Vorstershoop 30 Morokweng 43
Molopo 84 27 Voorspoed
Tshabong Ewbank 50
Crafthole
McCarthy's Rest

Heuningvlei

49

R380 **N o r t h   W e s t**

Middelputs 23 Severn 22
Aansluit 31 27
62 14
Khuis 5 Avontuur Maswehatshe
Molopo 15 16 33 Ditshipengo
Van Zylsrus 3 Takoon
R31 15 13 Tsineng Bothithongo 1823
64 51 54 Black Rock 13 Ga-Mopedi
31 Ontmoeting 21 Hotazel Lykso
Kuruman Sonstraal R31 132
Dedeben 61 Soeding Moffat's
Faans Grove Witloop R380 Mamathwane Mission Mothibistat N14
KORANNABERG 1550m 29 50 Kuruman 13
Sutton 20 Vlermuisvlakte 52 Eye of 16 R31 R372 66
23 26 Wincanton Kuruman
Markramsdraai 9 18 Bekker
45 15 Dibeng 42 R373 Blikfontein 32
12 Kathu 58 1855m
War 35 Sishen 12 Wonderwerk R31
Graves 41 Caves
1897 Moeswal Langkloof Droespruit Mookaneng Danielskuil Swartputs
War Graves 1877 24 Langberg Lohatlha 52
Olifantshoek 5 Lohatlha
Vroeggedeel 21
160 N14 Vrolik Glosam 31
56 R385 Palingpan
Bokkoppie
Blinkklip

22° To Upington 23° To Postmasburg 24°

5   6   12   7   8

Copyright ©Map Studio

o r t h e r n   C a p e

KURUMAN HILLS

To Vryburg

20

A

B

26°

C

20

27°

D

E

28°

Capital or City
Chief Administrative Town
Major Town

◉ Secondary Town
⊙ Other Town
○ Settlement

✈ Major Airport
Airfield
Accommodation

• Place of Interest
★ Historical Site
◄ Border Control

Ⓣ Toll Route
Ⓣ Toll Plaza
▲ Major Spot Height

Game & Nature Reserves
Marsh
Waterfall

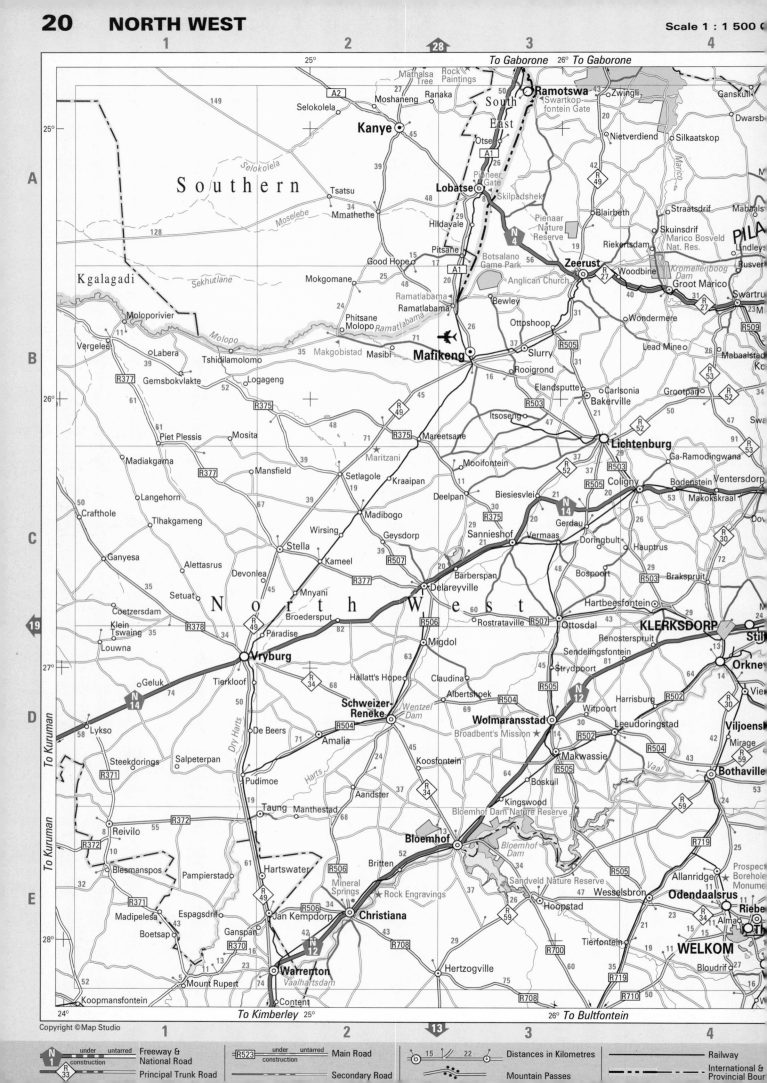

To Burgersfort   To Ohrigstad   To Satara

Kennedy's Vale
Glen Cowie
Geological Exposure
R555
Buffelsvlei
Joubertbrug
Pilgrims Rest
Graskop
R533
R534
R535
Bushbuckridge
Newington
Mala Mala
Londolozi
Tshokwane
Orpen Dam
Macaena
Massintonto

Krugerspost
R533
Ohrigstad Dam N.R.
Kowyn Pass
Marite
Sabi-Sabi
Jakkalsbessie
R569

Maartenshoop
Lydenburg
R37
Mauchsberg
Ohrigstad Dam
R536
Hazyview
Paul Kruger Gate
H11
Bushveld Camp
H10
15

De Berg Pass
Erts
R577
Roossenekal
Sabie
Long Long Pass
Kiepersol
S1
Skukuza
H1-1
H4-1
Lower Sabie
Machatuine
Chinhanguanine
Sabieo

Klipskool
Hendriksdal
R538
R537
Witrivier
Numbi Gate
Pretoriuskop
Jock of the Bushveld
H1-2

R555
Laersdrift
Sudwala Caves
R539
Brondal
Plaston
KaNyamazane
Berg-en-dal
H3
Afsaal
Crocodile Bridge
Komatipoort
Lebombo
Ressano Garcia

A

R540
Dullstroom
R36
Kwena Dam
Schoemanskloof
Elands River Valley
NELSPRUIT
Karino
Mthethomusha Game Res.
Hectorspruit
Malelane Gate
Malelane
N4
Komati
Machatuine

Belfast
Dalmanutha
Waterval-Boven
N4
Krugerhof
N.Z.A.S.M. Tunnel
Kaapsehoop
Noordkaap
Kaapmuiden
Kaalrug
Incomati
Moamba
Vundica

To Witbank
Wonderfontein
R541
Bothasnek
Nelshoogte
Jambila
First Stock Exchange
Avoca
Hhohho
Jeppe's Reef
Matsomo
R570
SEE PAGES 66-67
R571
LEBOMBOBERG
EN4
Pessene
Marracu

B

Machadodorp
Mineral Springs Badplaas
R541
Barberton
Saddleback
Bulembu
Josefsdal
Songimvelo Game Res.
Ngonini
Herefords
Piggs Peak
Sihhoye
Mananga
Sand River Reservoir
Lomahasha
Tjaneni
Mhlume
Namaacha
EN251
EN5
EN2
Matola
Machava
Boane

Carolina
R36
R38
Lochiel
Malolotja Nat. Res.
Bushman Paintings
Croydon
Bhalekane
Vuvulane
Tambankulu
Mlawula
Goba
Mnjoli Dam
Maputo

Chrissiesmeer
N17
Warburton
Hartbeeskop
Oshoek
R33
Forbes Reef
Simunye
Mlawula Nature Reserve
Changalane
Bela Vista

Breyten
R36
Lothair
Waverley
Lundzi
MBABANE
Swazi Market
Mbuluzi
Mpaka
Siteki
Lubombo

C

N11
Ermelo
Holbank
Bankkop
Amsterdam
Nerston
Sandlane
Lusutfu
Bushman Paintings
Mhlambanyatsi
Malkerns
Bhunya
Loyengo
Mankayane
MANZINI
Mafutseni
Sidvokodvo
Sipofaneni
Lubhuku
Mkhaya N.R.
MOÇAMBIQ

Sheepmoor
Iswepe
Ngwempisi
Bushman Paintings
Emahlatini
SWAZILAND
Ngwempisi
Big Bend
Catuane

21

Mpumalanga
Sicunusa
Mineral Baths
Gege
Kubutsa
Sithobela
Ndumo Game Reserve
Tembe Elephant Reserve
Lake Sibaya

Piet Retief
Anysspruit
Bothashoop
Nhlangano
Hlatsikhulu
Maloma
Nsoko
Cecil Macks Pass
Ingwavuma
Ndumo

R543
Wittenberg
R33
Mahamba
Mhlosheni
Hluthi
Lavumisa
Pongola

D

Latemanek
Dirkiesdorp
Berbice
Onverwacht
Golela
Golela
Kingholm
Candover
Jozini
Pongolapoort Nature Reserve
Mbaswa

Wakkerstroom
Braunschweig
Luneberg
Commondale
N2
Pongola
Pongolapoort Dam

Groenvlei
Grootspruit
Paulpietersburg
Itala Nature Reserve
Magudu
Louwsburg
R66
Nkoakonini
SEE PAGES 62-63
Ubombo
Mkuzi Game Reserve

BALELESBERG
2277m
Bivane
Pongola
Bivane
Ubombo
Mkuze
Phinda Resource Reserve

N11
Utrecht
Mpemvana
Hot Springs
Zungwini
P.L. Uys Memorial
Mkuze
Bayala
St. L
The Greater St. Lucia We

Madadeni
Ozizweni
Kingsley
Hlobane
Alpha
R601
Ngome
Thokazi
Nongoma
Leven Poi

E

Ballengeich
Bloedrivier
R34
Steilrand
Vryheid
Raadsaal and Fort of New Republic
Swart Umfolozi
Phinda Resource Reserve

Dannhauser
Calvert
Gluckstadt
Kwaceza
Hluhluwe Game Reserve
St. Lucia

Hattingspruit
Van Rooyen
Ntabebomvu
Prince Imperial 1879 Monument
SEE PAGES 62-63
Hluhluwe Umfolozi Dam
Hluhluwe

Fort Mistake
Dundee
SEE PAGES 64-65
Nondweni
R66
Hlabisa
Mahlabatini
Bushlands
Cape Vidal

Glencoe
Nqutu
Mahlabatini

To Ladysmith   To Ulundi   To Mtubatuba

Copyright © Map Studio

N1 — under construction / untarred — Freeway & National Road
R33 — Principal Trunk Road
R523 — under construction / untarred — Main Road
Secondary Road
15 / 22 — Distances in Kilometres
Mountain Passes
Railway
International & Provincial Bou

10 20 30 40 50km

5   6   31   7   8

33° To Chókwe   34°   To Quissico   35°

Malaira   Zandamela   *Lagoa Quissico*

Mazivila   Chissano   67   Madender

Lagoa   EN1   37   Chidenguele   *Lagoa Inhampavala*
Chuáli   30   45
17   31   Chongoene   *Lagoa Nhanzume*
avane*   25   13   Praia do
Macia   9   Chongoene   A
408   33   Xai-Xai   Praia do Xai-Xai

Incomáti   23

Praia do Bilene
Lagoa Uembje
nhiça
Lagoa Muandje
Lagoa Pati

INDIAN OCEAN

B

Ilha da Inhaca
Cabo de Santa Maria
Santa Maria

hangulo

Ponta Milibangalala   C

goa Piti

a do Ouro
a do Ouro
ay
ay Nature Reserve   27°
Point   D

nd Marine Reserve

Lion in the Kruger National Park

E

28°

5   6   7   8

Copyright ©Map Studio

Capital or City	Secondary Town	Major Airport	Place of Interest	Toll Route	Game & Nature Reserves
Chief Administrative Town	Other Town	Airfield	Historical Site	Toll Plaza	Marsh
Major Town	Settlement	Accommodation	Border Control	Major Spot Height	Waterfall

To Toscanini   To Uis Mine

National West Coast
Tourist Recreation Area
C34

116

Messum Crater

Omaruru

Omaruru River
Game Park

D1931

D2306
The Bull
(Group of

D3716

Cape Cross Bay
Seal Reserve
Cape Cross
Diego Cão's Cross

30

Rock Engravings *SPITZKOPPE*
★1759

D1930

E r o n g o

24

Aukas

46   102
C35

Ebony
Stingbank

Omaruru
C34
D1918
Omarurumund   6 7
Hentiesbaai

124   Waterbank
Khan
D1989

Trekkopje

National West Coast
Tourist Recreational Area

67

Arandis

CHUOSBERGE
D191

A T L A N T I C   O C E A N

Wlotzkasbaken
Rock Bay
C34

Rössing

Welwitschia P

Namib
Vineta
Swakopmund ⊙
Old Railway Station

B2

Martin Luther
Abandoned
Steam Tractor

D1991

Goanikontes

Swakop

B2
Walvis Bay
Pelican Point★
Old Rhenish Mission Church
Walvis Bay

Rand Rifles

34
Rooikop   C14

C28   155

D1982
161

D1983

C14

Sandwich Bay
Flamingoes
○ Sandwich Harbour

⌂○ Gobabeb

Kuiseb

H a r d a p

Conception Bay

N

Namib

Naukluft

Park

Flowers in the Namib

A
M

Meob Bay
Hollansbird Island ○

I

B

Fischersbrunn ○   Sossusvlei

To Toscanini   To Uis Mine

Copyright ©Map Studio

N1 / R33 under construction / untarred   Freeway & National Road

Principal Trunk Road

R523 under construction / untarred   Main Road

Secondary Road

15 22 Distances in Kilometres

Mountain Passes

Railway

International & Provincial Boun

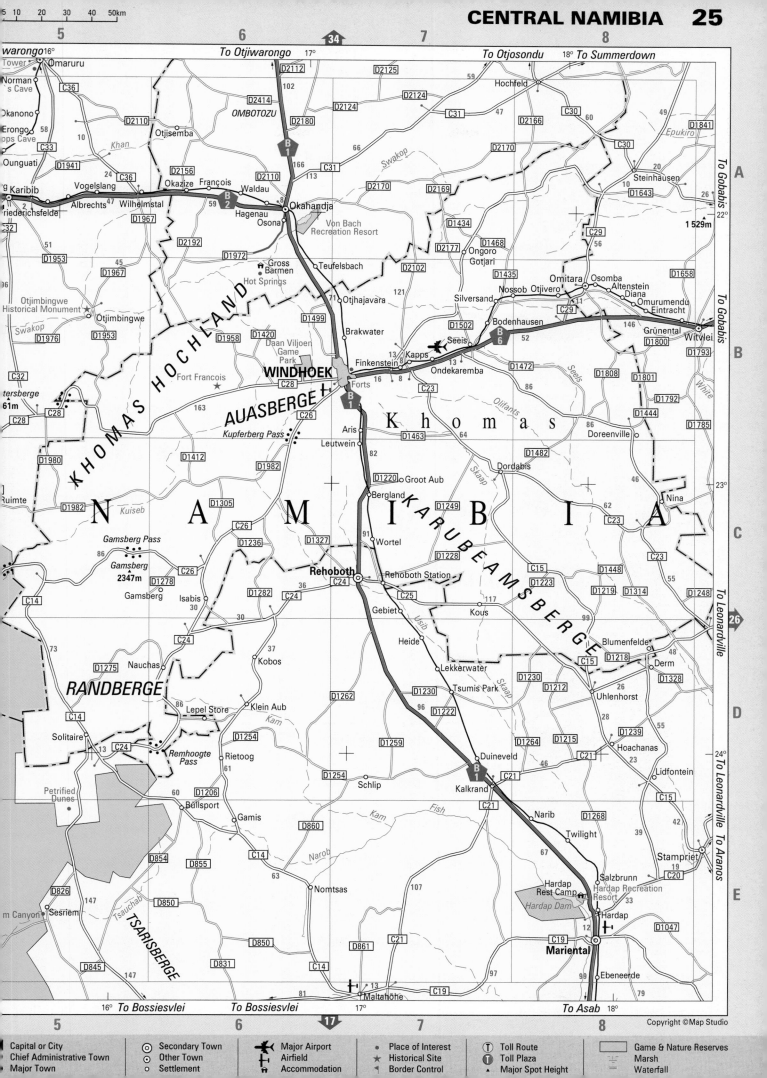

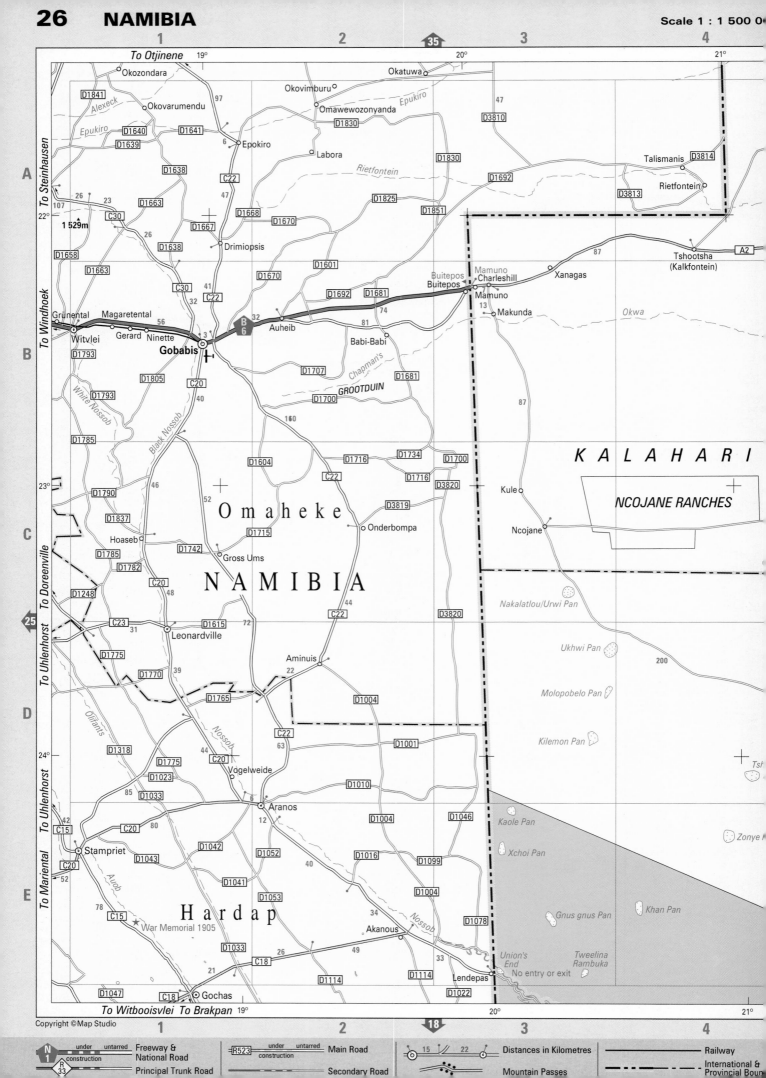

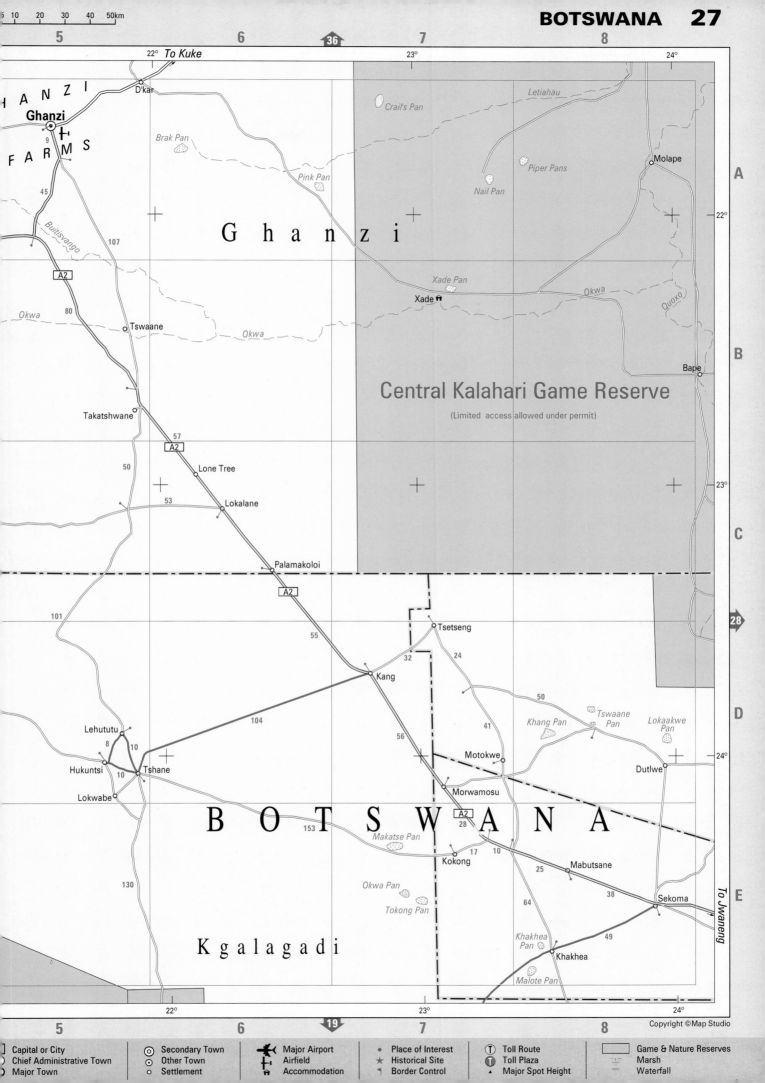

5 10 20 30 40 50km

22° *To Kuke*

D'kar

GHANZI
Ghanzi
9
FARMS
45

Brak Pan

Pink Pan

Crail's Pan

Letiahau

Piper Pans

Molape

A

22°

107

A2

80

Buitisvango

G h a n z i

Xade Pan

Xade

Okwa

Quoxo

Okwa

Tswaane

Okwa

B

Takatshwane

Central Kalahari Game Reserve

(Limited access allowed under permit)

Bape

57

A2

50

Lone Tree

53

Lokalane

C

23°

Palamakoloi

A2

101

28

Tsetseng

55

32

24

Kang

50

Tswaane Pan

Lokaakwe Pan

Lehututu

104

41

Khang Pan

D

8   10

Hukuntsi

10

Tshane

56

Motokwe

Dutlwe

24°

Lokwabe

Morwamosu

B O T S W A N A

A2

153

28

Makatse Pan

17   10

Kokong

25

Mabutsane

38

Okwa Pan

64

Sekoma

To Jwaneng

E

130

K g a l a g a d i

Tokong Pan

Khakhea Pan

49

Khakhea

Malote Pan

22°

23°

24°

19

Copyright ©Map Studio

Capital or City		Secondary Town		Major Airport		Place of Interest		Toll Route	Game & Nature Reserves
Chief Administrative Town		Other Town		Airfield		Historical Site		Toll Plaza	Marsh
Major Town		Settlement		Accommodation		Border Control		Major Spot Height	Waterfall

A

B

C

27

D

E

Central Kalahari Game Reserve
(Limited access allowed under permit)

Bape

Quoxo

Meratswe

Kutse Pan

Kutse
Game
Reserve

C e n t r a l

18 Letlhakane
Ditsinane Pan

107

Mmashoro

60

Thataganyana Rock
Mogorosi 16
Serowe

Kalamare

Chief's Grave and Mission Site 35
Shoshong

Mahalapy

40

Lehepe Pan
Lephepe

Sojwe

Dinok

48 27
Mmamabula

Dibete

66

46

Ngotwan

Tsia Salajwe

72

Tsesame
Khudumalapye 62

Takatokwane

81

Naledi

Letlhakeng

Kgari Pan

65

Moshaweng

Tshinka Pan

A2

88

Jwaneng

K w e n e n g

Botlhapatlou

11 *Ngwanche Pan*

Lentsweletau

48

Petrified
Forest

Livingstone's
Cave ★

Molepolole ★
Rock Engravings ★
Engravings ★
Kopong ★
50

46

Thamaga

Livingstone's
Mission

22

Mosopo

Mathalsa
Tree

Rock
Paintings

82

A2

27 Ranaka

Monametsana

56

K g a t l e n g

Malotwana
Rock Engravings

Pilane
8

Mochudi

43

A1
35

GABORONE ✈

Gabane
Tlokweng

Tlokweng 18

24 Kopfontein
Gate

40

52

Ramotswa
Swattkop

Sikwane

Medipane

*Madikwe
Game
Reserve*

Derdepoort

Kayaseput

25

Zwingli
99

Marico

Rooibe

Spa

Silent
Valley

Oost

Dwaalbom

Ganskull

24°

25° *To Kanye* *To Lobatse* 26° *To Zeerust*

22°

23°

24°

25°

26°

Copyright ©Map Studio

1 2 37 3 4

20

1 2 3 4

N 1 / **R 33** under construction / untarred	Freeway & National Road / Principal Trunk Road	
R523 under construction / untarred	Main Road	
	Secondary Road	
15 22	Distances in Kilometres	
	Mountain Passes	
	Railway	
	International & Provincial Bound	

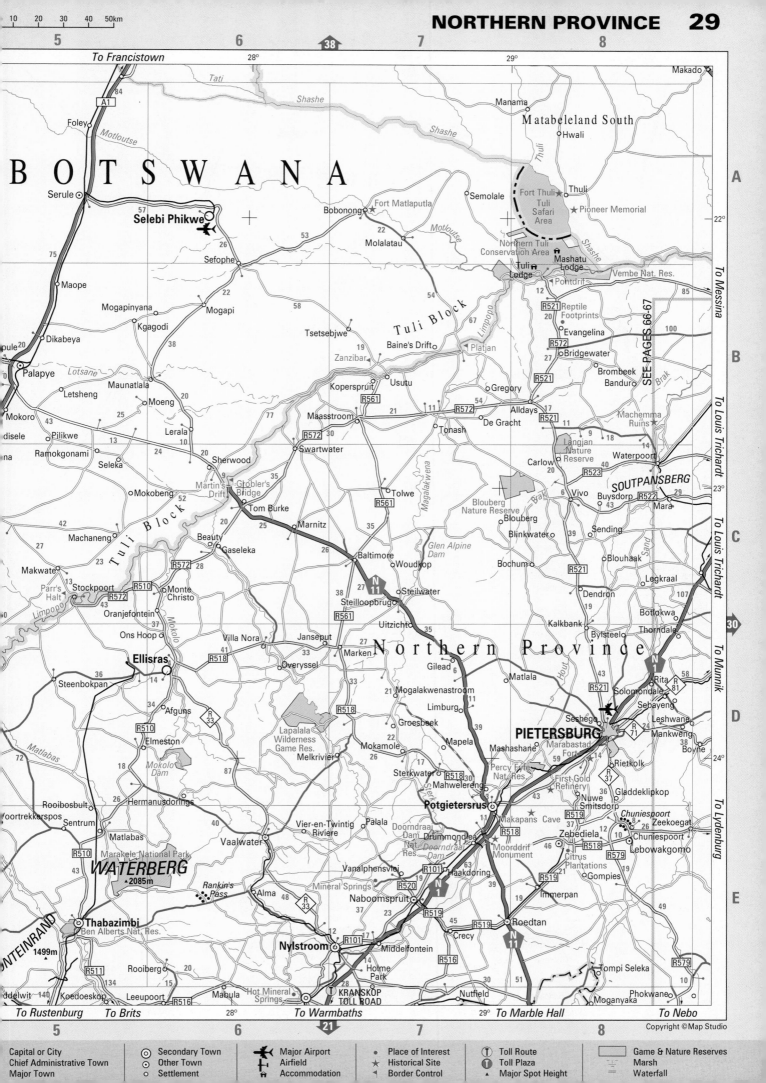

10 20 30 40 50km

To Francistown

BOTSWANA

Matabeleland South

Serule
Foley
A1
Selebi Phikwe
Maope
Mogapinyana
Kgagodi
Dikabeya
Palapye
Letsheng
Moeng
Maunatlala
Ramokgonami
Seleka
Pilikwe
Lerala
Makwate
Machaneng
Stockpoort
Mokobeng
Parr's Halt
Oranjefontein
Ons Hoop
Steenbokpan
Afguns
Elmeston
Rooibosbult
Sentrum
Matlabas
Thabazimbi
Ben Alberts Nat. Res.
Rooiberg
Koedoeskop
Leeuwpoort

Sefophe
Mogapi
Sherwood
Martin's Drift
Grobler's Bridge
Tom Burke
Beauty
Gaseleka
Monte Christo
Villa Nora
Ellisras
Vaalwater
Rankin's Pass
Alma
Mabula
Hot Mineral Springs
Nylstroom
Middelfontein
Holme Park
Koppies

Bobonong
Fort Matlaputla
Molalatau
Tsetsebjwe
Zanzibar
Baine's Drift
Kopersproit
Usutu
Maasstroom
Swartwater
Tolwe
Marnitz
Baltimore
Woudkop
Steilwater
Steiloopbrug
Uitzicht
Janseput
Marken
Overyssel
Gilead
Mogalakwenastroom
Limburg
Groesbeek
Mokamole
Melkrivier
Sterkwater
Mahwelereng
Potgietersrus
Palala
Vier-en-Twintig Riviere
Vanalphensvlei
Mineral Springs
Naboomspruit
Crecy

Tuli Block

Manama
Hwali
Fort Thuli
Tuli Safari Area
Pioneer Memorial
Semolale
Northern Tuli Conservation Area
Tuli Lodge
Mashatu Lodge
Pontdrift
Vembe Nat. Res.
Platjan
Gregory
Reptile Footprints
Evangelina
Bridgewater
Brombeek
Bandur
Alldays
De Gracht
Tonash
Carlow
Langjan Nature Reserve
Waterpoort
Soutpansberg
Vivo
Buysdorp
Mara
Sending
Blouberg
Blouberg Nature Reserve
Blinkwater
Bochum
Blouhaak
Legkraal
Dendron
Botlokwa
Thorndale
Kalkbank
Bysteel
Matlala
Solomondale
Rita
Sebayeng
Leshwane
Mankweng
Boyne
PIETERSBURG
Seshego
Marabastad Fort
Rietkolk
Percy Fyfe Nat. Res.
Mashashane
First Gold Refinery
Nuwe Smitsdorp
Gladdeklipkop
Mapela
Makapans Cave
Zebediela
Chuniespoort
Zeekoegat
Lebowakgomo
Citrus Plantations
Gompies
Immerpan
Roedtan
Tompi Seleka
Phokwane
Moganyaka

Northern Province

WATERBERG
▲2085m
Lapalala Wilderness Game Res.
Marakele National Park

Mokolo Dam
Doornpraai Dam Nat. Res.
Doorndraai Dam
Drummondlea
Moorddrif Monument
Haakdoring

To Rustenburg   To Brits   To Warmbaths   To Marble Hall   To Nebo

To Messina
To Louis Trichardt
To Munnik
To Lydenburg

SEE PAGES 66-67

Capital or City
Chief Administrative Town
Major Town

◎ Secondary Town
⊙ Other Town
○ Settlement

✈ Major Airport
✈ Airfield
⌂ Accommodation

• Place of Interest
★ Historical Site
◄ Border Control

Ⓣ Toll Route
Ⓣ Toll Plaza
▲ Major Spot Height

Game & Nature Reserves
Marsh
Waterfall

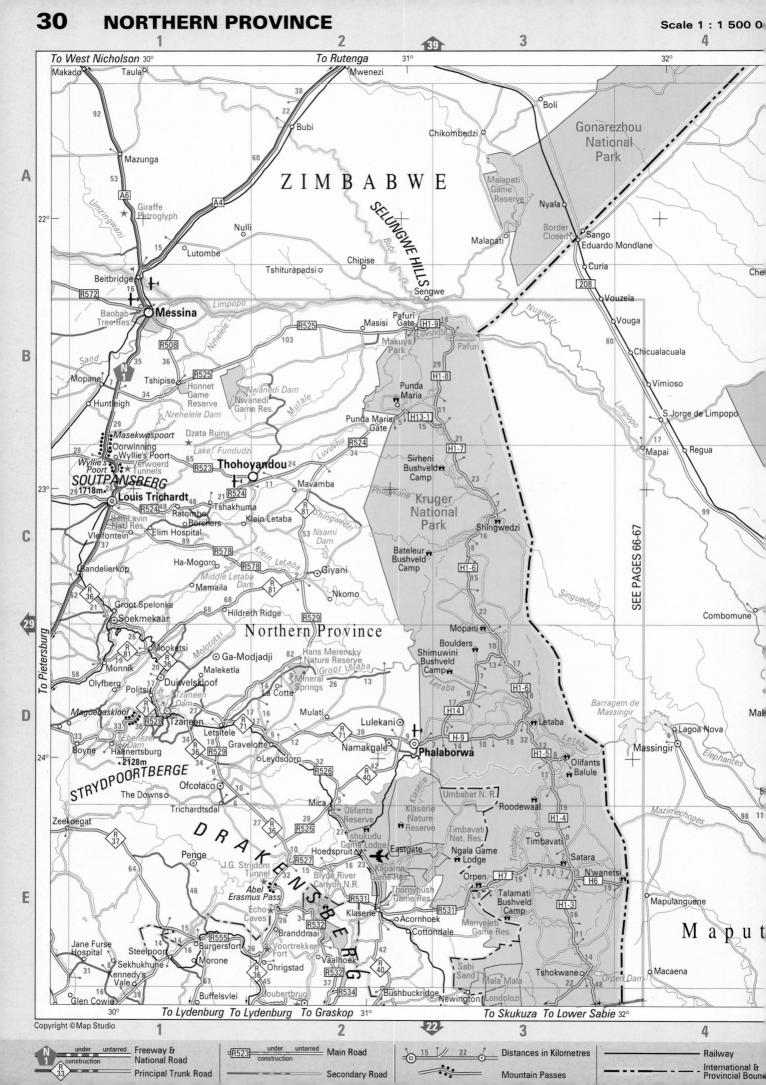

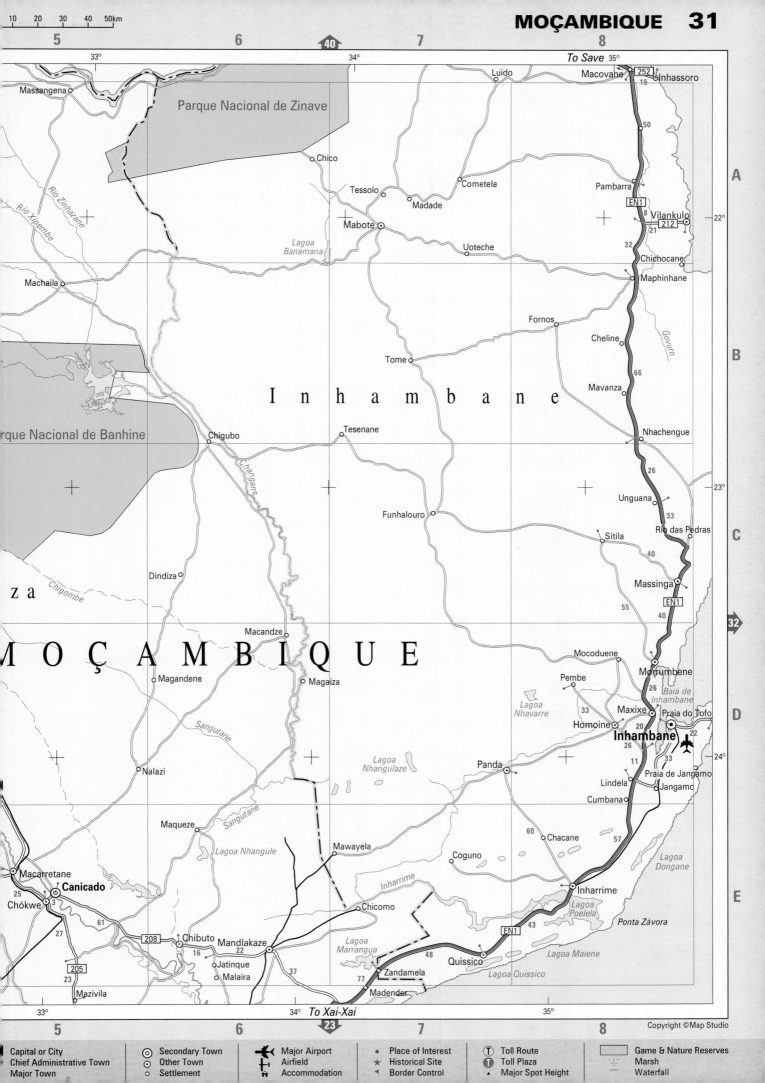

Parque Nacional de Zinave

Parque Nacional de Banhine

Parque Nacional de Banhine

Inhambane

MOÇAMBIQUE

To Save

To Xai-Xai

Massangena
Chico
Luido
Macovane
Inhassoro
Tessolo
Cometela
Pambarra
Madade
Vilankulo
Mabote
Chichocane
Uoteche
Maphinhane
Machaila
Fornos
Cheline
Tome
Mavanza
Nhachengue
Chigubo
Tesenane
Unguana
Funhalouro
Sitila
Rio das Pedras
Dindiza
Massinga
Macandze
Mocoduene
Magandene
Magaiza
Pembe
Morrumbene
Maxixe
Praia do Tofo
Homoine
Inhambane
Nalazi
Panda
Lindela
Praia de Jangamo
Jangamo
Cumbana
Maqueze
Chacane
Mawayela
Macarretane
Coguno
Canicado
Inharrime
Chókwe
Chibuto
Mandlakaze
Jatinque
Quissico
Malaira
Zandamela
Mazivila
Madender

Rio Zinhazane
Rio Xipembe
Lagoa Banamana
Govuro
Changane
Chigombe
Sangutane
Sangutane
Lagoa Nhavarre
Baiá de Inhambane
Lagoa Nhangulaze
Lagoa Nhangule
Inharrime
Lagoa Dongane
Lagoa Poelela
Lagoa Marrangua
Lagoa Quissico
Lagoa Maiene
Ponta Závora

EN1
EN1
EN1
EN1
252
212
208
205
40
23

10 20 30 40 50km

Copyright ©Map Studio

Capital or City
Chief Administrative Town
Major Town
Secondary Town
Other Town
Settlement
Major Airport
Airfield
Accommodation
Place of Interest
Historical Site
Border Control
Toll Route
Toll Plaza
Major Spot Height
Game & Nature Reserves
Marsh
Waterfall

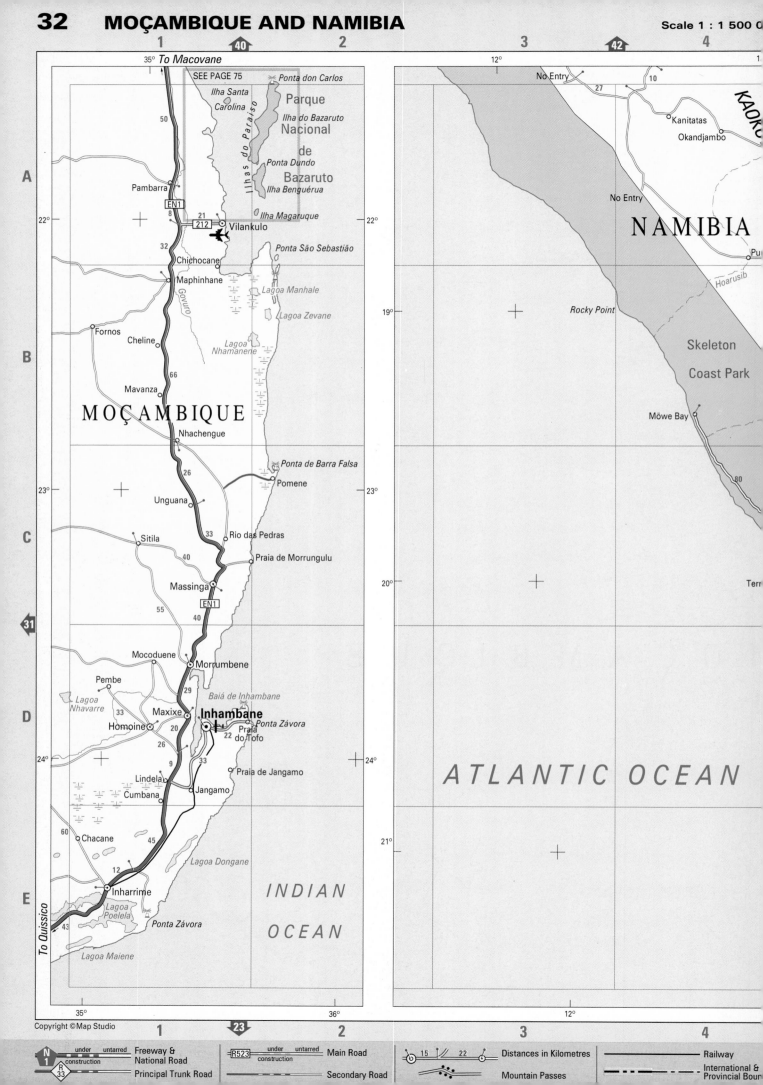

Parque Nacional de Bazaruto

To Macovane

SEE PAGE 75

Ponta don Carlos
Ilha Santa Carolina
Ilha do Bazaruto
Ponta Dundo
Ilha Benguérua
Ilha Magaruque
Ponta São Sebastião

Pambarra
EN1
Vilankulo
Chichocane
Maphinhane
Lagoa Manhale
Lagoa Zevane
Govuro
Fornos
Cheline
Lagoa Nhamanene
Mavanza

MOÇAMBIQUE

Nhachengue
Ponta de Barra Falsa
Pomene
Unguana
Rio das Pedras
Sitila
Praia de Morrungulu
Massinga
EN1

Mocoduene
Morrumbene
Pembe
Baiá de Inhambane
Lagoa Nhavarre
Maxixe
Inhambane
Homoine
Ponta Závora
Praia do Tofo
Lindela
Praia de Jangamo
Cumbana
Jangamo
Chacane
Lagoa Dongane
Inharrime

To Quissico
Lagoa Poelela
Ponta Závora
Lagoa Maiene

INDIAN OCEAN

NAMIBIA

No Entry
Kanitatas
Okandjambo
No Entry
Pu
Hoarusib
Rocky Point
Skeleton Coast Park
Möwe Bay
Terr

ATLANTIC OCEAN

Copyright © Map Studio

	under construction	untarred			under construction	untarred				
N1			Freeway & National Road	R523			Main Road	15 22	Distances in Kilometres	Railway
R33			Principal Trunk Road				Secondary Road		Mountain Passes	International & Provincial Bour

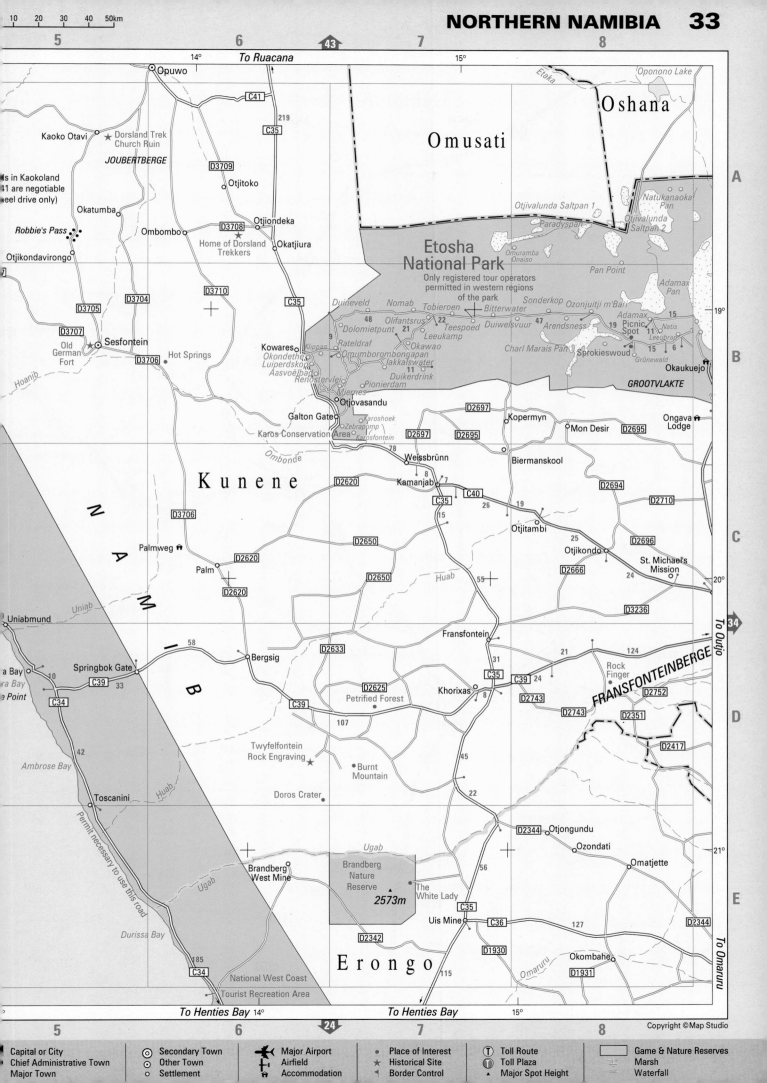

10 20 30 40 50km

5   6   43   7   8

To Ruacana

Opuwo

C41

219

C35

Kaoko Otavi   ★ Dorsland Trek
                Church Ruin
JOUBERTBERGE

Ms in Kaokoland
41 are negotiable
eel drive only)

Okatumba

Robbie's Pass

Otjikondavirongo

Otjitoko

Ombombo

D3709

Otjiondeka

D3708

Okatjiura
Home of Dorsland
Trekkers

D3704   D3710   C35

D3705

D3707

Old
German Fort   ★ Sesfontein

D3706

Hot Springs

Hoanib

Kowares

Okondethe
Luiperdskop
Aasvoëlbad
Renostervlei
Viernes
Otjovasandu

Galton Gate

Karos Conservation Area

Klippan
Rateldraf
Omumborombongapan
Jakkalswater
Duikerdrink
Pionierdam

Karoshoek
Zebrapomp
Karosfontein

Ombonde

78

Weissbrünn

Omusati

Oshana

Otjivalunda Saltpan 1

Paradyspan

Oponono Lake

Natukanaoka
Pan

*Otjivalunda
Saltpan 2*

**Etosha
National Park**
Only registered tour operators
permitted in western regions
of the park

*Omuramba
Onaiso*

Pan Point

Duineveld   *Nomab*   Tobieroen
48   Olifantsrus   22   *Bitterwater*
Dolomietpunt   21   Teespoed   *Duiwelsvuur*
9   Okawao   Leeukamp
11   Duikerdrink

Sonderkop   Ozonjuitji m'Bari
47   Arendsness
19

Charl Marais Pan

Adamax
Pan

15
Adamax
Picnic   11   Natis
Spot   Leeubrap
15   6

Sprokieswoud   *Grünewald*

Okaukuejo

GROOTVLAKTE

D2697

D2697   D2695

Kopermyn

Mon Desir

Ongava
Lodge

D2695

K u n e n e

D2620

Kamanjab

8   7
C35   C40

15

D2650

Biermanskool

19

Otjitambi

26

D2694

D2710

25

D2696

Otjikondo

24

St. Michael's
Mission

D2666

D3236

N

D3706

Palmweg

Palm

D2620

D2620

D2650

Huab

55

20°

To Oujo   34

A

B

C

Uniab

Uniabmund

A
M
I
B

58

Bergsig

D2633

Fransfontein

31

21   124

Rock
Finger

FRANSFONTEINBERGE

D2752

a Bay
a Bay
e Point

10

C39   33

C34

Springbok Gate

C39

D2625
Petrified Forest

C39

Khorixas

C35   C39   24
8
D2743

D2743

D2351

D2417

D

107

42

Ambrose Bay

Toscanini

Huab

Twyfelfontein
Rock Engraving ★

Burnt
Mountain

Doros Crater

45

22

D2344   Otjongundu

Ozondati

Omatjette

21°

Durissa Bay

Ugab

Brandberg
West Mine

**Brandberg
Nature
Reserve**
▲
The White Lady
2573m

D2342

56

Uis Mine   C35

C36

D1930

115

185
C34

National West Coast
Tourist Recreation Area

E r o n g o

Omaruru

Okombahe

127   D2344

D1931

E

To Henties Bay   14°

To Henties Bay   15°

24

To Omaruru

5   6   7   8

Copyright ©Map Studio

◉ Capital or City	◎ Secondary Town	✈ Major Airport	• Place of Interest	ⓣ Toll Route	▢ Game & Nature Reserves
Chief Administrative Town	◉ Other Town	⊕ Airfield	★ Historical Site	ⓣ Toll Plaza	Marsh
Major Town	○ Settlement	⌂ Accommodation	Border Control	▲ Major Spot Height	Waterfall

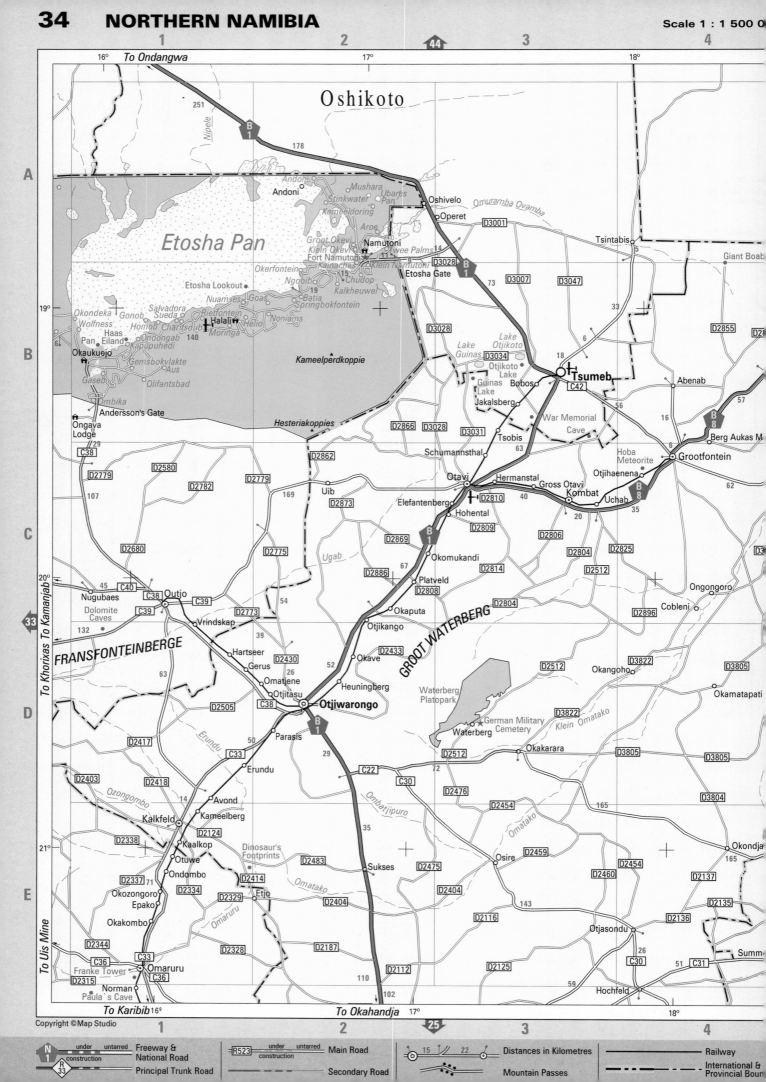

To Ondangwa

Oshikoto

Etosha Pan

Andoni
Mushara
Stinkwater
Pan
Kameeldoring
Ubares
Pan
Aroe
Oshivelo
Operet
D3001
Tsintabis
Giant Boab

Groot Okevi
Klein Okevi
Namutoni
Twee Palms
Okerfonteine
Kainachas
Fort Namutoni
Klein Namutoni
Etosha Gate
D3028
D3007
D3047
Etosha Lookout
Ngobib
Chudop
Kalkheuwel
Nuamses
Goas
Batia
Springbokfontein
D3028
Lake Otjikoto
Okondeka
Salvadora
Rietfontein
Moringa
Helio
Noniams
Lake Guinas
D3034
Otjikoto Lake
D2855
Wolfness
Gonob
Sueda
Homob
Charitsoub
Ondongab
Halali
Guinas Lake
Guinas
18
Tsumeb
C42
Abenab
Haas
Pan Eiland
Kapupuhedi
140
Jakalsberg
Boboso
Okaukuejo
Gemsbokvlakte
Aus
Gaseb
Olifantsbad
Kameelperdkoppie
War Memorial Cave
16
Berg Aukas M
57
Ombika
Andersson's Gate
Hesteriakoppies
D2866
D3028
D3031
Tsobis
63
Berg Aukas M
Ongava Lodge
29
C38
D2862
Schumannsthal
Hoba Meteorite
Grootfontein
D2779
D2580
D2782
D2779
Otavi
Hermanstal
Gross Otavi
Otjihaenena
62
D2779
169
Uib
D2873
Elefantenberg
D2810
Kombat
Uchab
35
C38
Outjo
C39
Okomukandi
Hohental
D2809
D2806
D2804
D2825
D3
D2680
D2775
D2886
67
Platveld
D2814
D2512
Ugab
D2808
Okaputa
D2804
Ongongoro
Nugubaes
C40
C38
45
Vrindskap
D2773
Otjikango
Cobleni
D2896
Dolomite Caves
C39
54
39
Okave
D2433
GROOT WATERBERG
Okangoho
D3822
D3805
132
Hartseer
D2430
52
Okamatapati
FRANSFONTEINBERGE
Gerus
26
Heuningberg
Waterberg Platopark
63
Omatjene
Otjitasu
German Military Cemetery
Otjiwarongo
C38
Waterberg
D3822
D2505
D2417
Parasis
Okakarara
D3805
D3805
50
C33
29
Erundu
C22
72
D2476
D2454
165
D3804
D2403
D2418
Ozongombo
14
Avond
C30
D2475
Kameelberg
35
D2459
Osire
D2454
D2137
Kalkfeld
D2124
Dinosaur's Footprints
D2483
Sukses
Okondja
165
D2338
Kaalkop
Suksesg
143
D2460
D2135
D2337
71
Otuwe
D2414
Etjo
D2404
D2116
Otjasondu
D2136
Okozongoro
D2334
D2329
Epako
Okakombo
D2125
26
To Uis Mine
D2344
C36
C33
D2328
D2187
D2112
59
51
C30
C31
Franke Tower
C36
Omaruru
110
102
Hochfeld
Summ
Norman Paula`s Cave
D2315

To Karibib
To Okahandja

under	untarred	
construction		Freeway & National Road

Principal Trunk Road

Main Road

Secondary Road

Distances in Kilometres

Mountain Passes

Railway

International & Provincial Boun

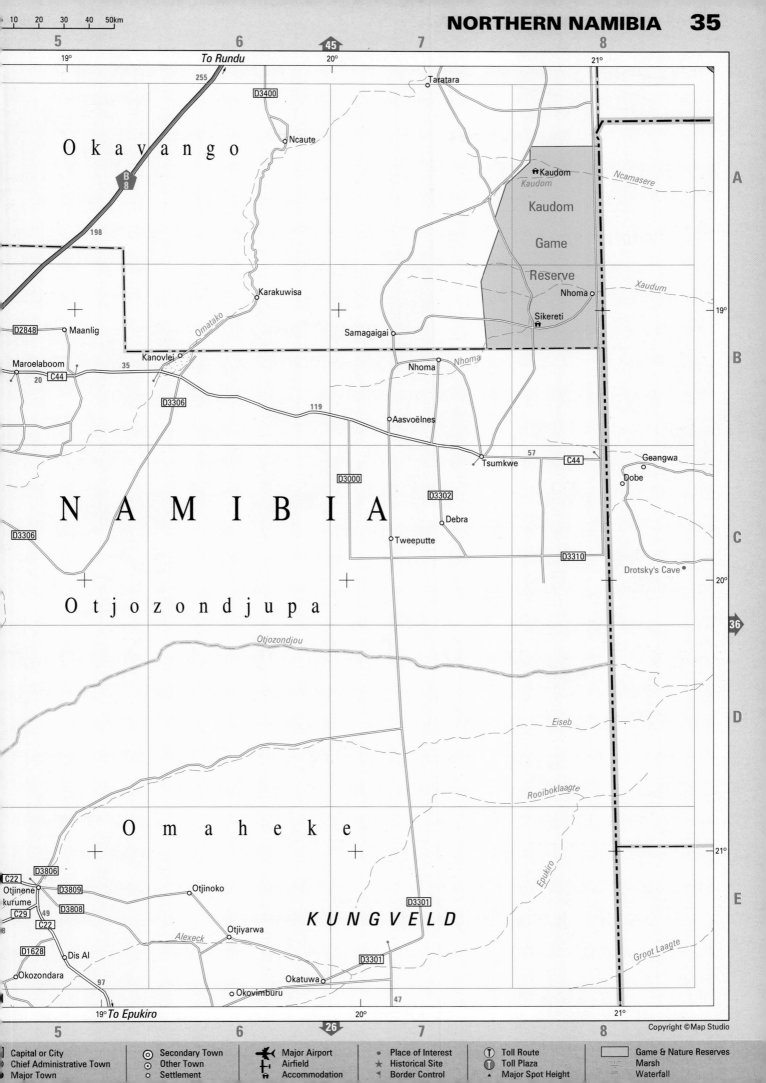

10 20 30 40 50km

To Rundu

19°   20°   21°

255

D3400

Taratara

O k a v a n g o

Ncaute

B8

Kaudom

Kaudom

Ncamasere

A

198

Kaudom

Game

Karakuwisa

Reserve

Nhoma

Xaudum

D2848 Maanlig

Samagaigai

Sikereti

19°

B

Maroelaboom

Kanovlei

Nhoma

Nhoma

C44

20

35

D3306

119

Aasvoëlnes

N A M I B I A

57

Geangwa

Tsumkwe C44

Dobe

D3000

D3302

D3306

Debra

Tweeputte

D3310

Drotsky's Cave

20°

C

O t j o z o n d j u p a

36

Otjozondjou

Eiseb

D

Rooiboklaagte

21°

O m a h e k e

C22 D3806

Otjinene

D3809 Otjinoko

Epukiro

kurume

D3301

C29 D3808

E

C22

K U N G V E L D

Otjiyarwa

Alexeck

D1628 Dis Al

Groot Laagte

Okozondara

97

Okatuwa

Okovimburu

47

Copyright ©Map Studio

Capital or City	Secondary Town	Major Airport	Place of Interest
Chief Administrative Town	Other Town	Airfield	Historical Site
Major Town	Settlement	Accommodation	Border Control

Toll Route
Toll Plaza
Major Spot Height

Game & Nature Reserves
Marsh
Waterfall

Scale 1 : 1 500 0

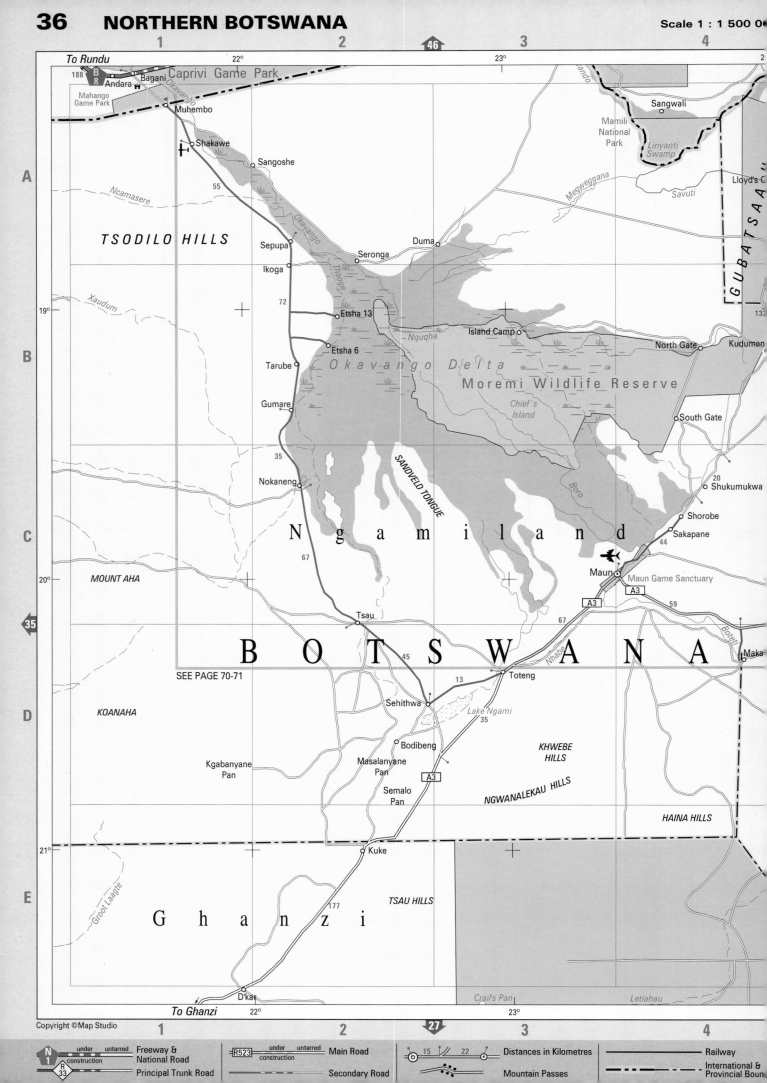

Scale: 10 20 30 40 50km

To Kazunga · **To Victoria Falls**

To Bulawayo · To Main Camp

To Francistown

To Serowe

Places and features

Kachekabwe
Ngwezumba
Kashaba
Ngwezumba
DEPRESSION
Chobe National Park
C h o b e
Kazuma Pan National Park
Mpandamatenga
Matetsi
Matetsi
106
Zambezi Deka · Deka
Hwange
A8
156
17
Robins Camp
Sinamatella
Pongore
Dete
Deka
Matetsi Safari Area
Shumba
Lukosi
100
20
19°
Hwange National Park
ZIMBABWE
180
Libuti Camp
Nxai Pan National Park
Nxai Pan
Kanyu
Bains Baobab
Matima · Phuduhudu
528 · 205
A3
Gweta
99
Nata
Nata
Sepako
Tsuli
20°
38
MAKGADIKGADI
B O T S W A N A
Kwaraga
Xhumaga
Dikwalo
Tsoe
Makgadikgadi Pans Game Reserve
Ntwetwe Pan
Sowa
Dukwe
Mosetse
180
Sowa Pan
21°
...akops · Mmadikola
54
A3
Mabe
Mopipi
60
Mopipi Pan
Gidikwe · Kaokare
Lake Xau
60
Orapa
18
Letlhakane
Mmatshumo
C e n t r a l
232
Mokobela Pan
Thakadu
Tlalamabele
Ditsinane Pan

Copyright ©Map Studio

Legend

Capital or City	Secondary Town	Major Airport
Chief Administrative Town	Other Town	Airfield
Major Town	Settlement	Accommodation

Place of Interest	Toll Route
Historical Site	Toll Plaza
Border Control	Major Spot Height

Game & Nature Reserves
Marsh
Waterfall

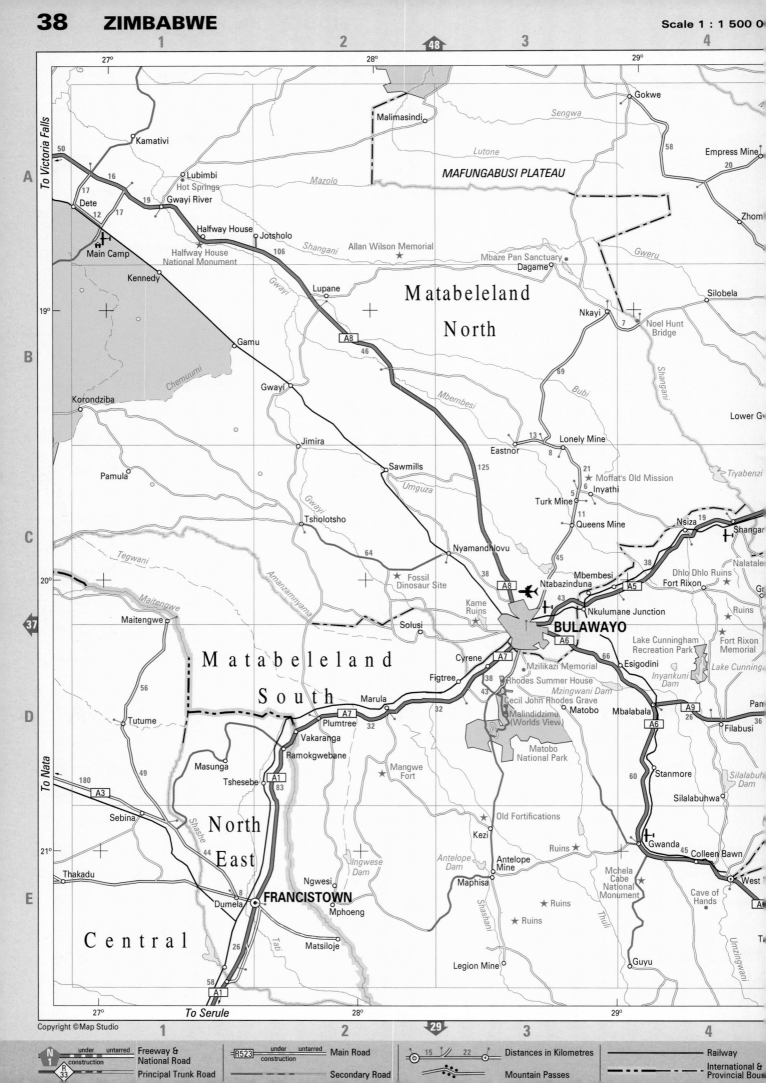

Legend:

N1 under construction / untarred	Freeway & National Road	Distances in Kilometres
R33	Principal Trunk Road	Mountain Passes
R523 under construction / untarred	Main Road	Railway
	Secondary Road	International & Provincial Boun

Map labels:

To Victoria Falls

27° 28° 48 29°

A
Kamativi
Malimasindi
MAFUNGABUSI PLATEAU
Gokwe
Sengwa
Lutone
Mazolo
Empress Mine
50
16
17
Lubimbi Hot Springs
19
Gwayi River
Dete
12 17
58 20
Zhom
Mbaze Pan Sanctuary
Dagame

B
Main Camp
Halfway House
Halfway House National Monument
Jotsholo
106
Shangani
Allan Wilson Memorial ★
Gweru
Silobela
Kennedy
Lupane
A8
46
19°
Matabeleland North
Nkayi
7
Noel Hunt Bridge
Gamu
Chemuumi
Gwayi
Gwayi
69
Bubi
Shangani
Korondziba
Jimira
Mbembesi
13
Lonely Mine
Lower G
Pamula
Eastnor
8
Tiyabenzi
Sawmills
125
21
Moffat's Old Mission ★
Gwayi
Umguza
6
Inyathi
Turk Mine
5

C
Tsholotsho
64
11
Queens Mine
Nsiza
19
Shangan
Tegwani
Nyamandhlovu
45
38
A8
Mbembesi
Dhlo Dhlo Ruins ★
Fort Rixon
Nalatale
20°
Amanzamnyama
Fossil Dinosaur Site ★
43
Ntabazinduna
Nkulumane Junction
A5
Gr
Ruins

D
37
Maitengwe
Maitengwe
Kame Ruins
BULAWAYO
A6
Lake Cunningham Recreation Park
Fort Rixon Memorial
Lake Cunning
Matabeleland South
Solusi
Cyrene
A7
Mzilikazi Memorial
66
Esigodini
Inyankuni Dam
56
Figtree
38
Rhodes Summer House
43
Cecil John Rhodes Grave
Matobo
Mbalabala
A9
Pan
Tutume
Marula
32
Mzingwani Dam
Malindidzimu (Worlds View)
A6
26
Filabusi
36
Plumtree
32
Matobo National Park
Vakaranga
Ramokgwebane
Masunga
A1
Stanmore
Silalabuh
Dam
Tshesebe
83
60
Silalabuhwa

E
To Nata
180
A3
49
Old Fortifications ★
Sebina
North East
Kezi
Ruins ★
Gwanda
45
Colleen Bawn
21°
44
Thakadu
Ingwese Dam
Antelope Dam
Antelope Mine
Ruins ★
West
A
8
Dumela
FRANCISTOWN
Ngwesi
Maphisa
Mchela Cabe National Monument
Cave of Hands
Shashani
Ruins ★
Mphoeng
26
Central
Matsiloje
Ruins ★
Legion Mine
Guyu
Ta
Umzingwani
58
A1
Tati
27° To Serule 29 28° 29°

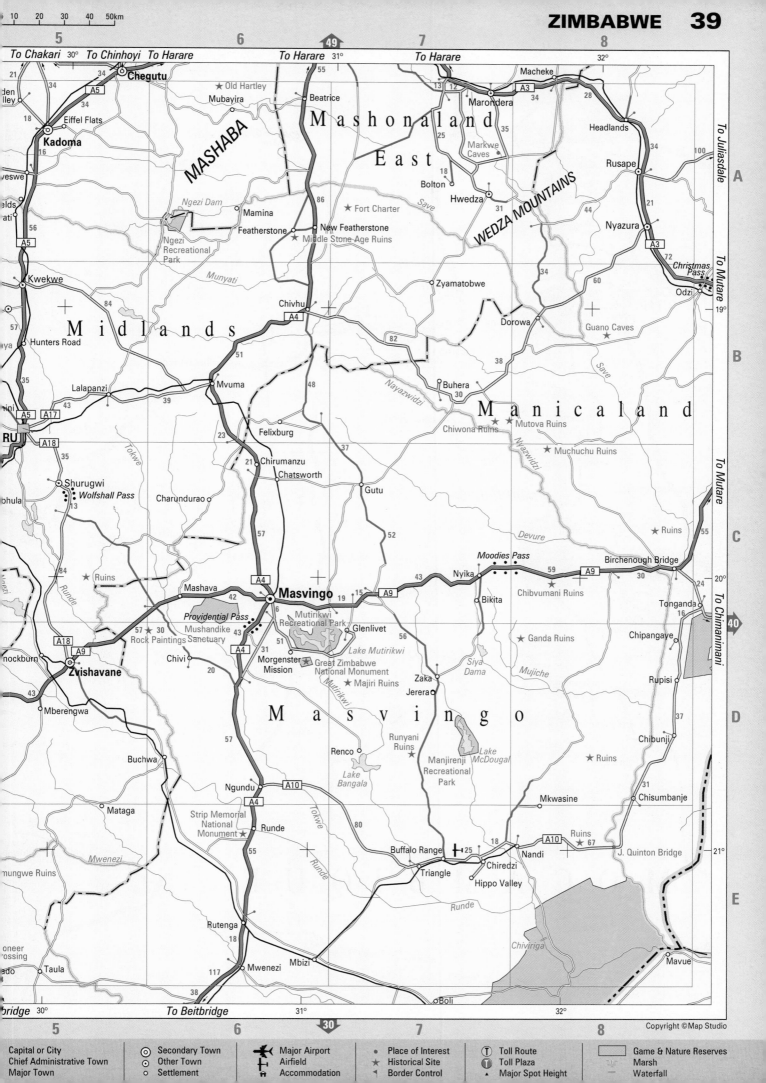

Map scale: 10 20 30 40 50km

Towns and places (by region):

MASHABA
Chegutu, Eiffel Flats, Kadoma, Mubayira, Old Hartley, Beatrice

Mashonaland East
Macheke, Marondera, Markwe Caves, Headlands, Rusape, Mamina, Fort Charter, Featherstone, New Featherstone, Middle Stone Age Ruins, Bolton, Hwedza, Nyazura, Zyamatobwe, Christmas Pass, Odzi

WEDZA MOUNTAINS

Midlands
Kwekwe, Hunters Road, Lalapanzi, Mvuma, Felixburg, Chirumanzu, Chatsworth, Charundurao, Shurugwi, Wolfshall Pass, Gutu, Dorowa, Guano Caves, Buhera

Manicaland
Chiwona Ruins, Mutova Ruins, Muchuchu Ruins, Ruins, Birchenough Bridge, Moodies Pass, Nyika, Chibvumani Ruins, Tonganda, Chipangaye, Rupisi, Chibunji, Ruins

Masvingo
Mashava, Masvingo, Providential Pass, Mushandike Sanctuary, Rock Paintings, Chivi, Zvishavane, Mberengwa, Buchwa, Mataga, Glenlivet, Morgenster Mission, Great Zimbabwe National Monument, Majiri Ruins, Lake Mutirikwi, Mutirikwi Recreational Park, Bikita, Ganda Ruins, Zaka, Jerera, Siya Dama, Mujiche, Renco, Runyani Ruins, Lake Bangala, Manjirenji Recreational Park, Lake McDougal, Ngundu, Strip Memorial National Monument, Runde, Mkwasine, Chisumbanje, Buffalo Range, Nandi, J. Quinton Bridge, Triangle, Chiredzi, Hippo Valley, Ruins, Rutenga, Mwenezi, Mbizi, Boli, Taula, Mavue, Chiviriga

Roads: A3, A4, A5, A9, A10, A17, A18

Rivers/features: Ngezi Dam, Ngezi Recreational Park, Munyati, Munyati, Tokwe, Save, Nyazwidzi, Nayazwidzi, Devure, Runde, Mwenezi, Mutirikwi

Copyright © Map Studio

Legend:
- Capital or City
- Chief Administrative Town
- Major Town
- ◎ Secondary Town
- ⊙ Other Town
- ○ Settlement
- ✈ Major Airport
- Airfield
- ⌂ Accommodation
- • Place of Interest
- ★ Historical Site
- Border Control
- Ⓣ Toll Route
- Ⓣ Toll Plaza
- ▲ Major Spot Height
- Game & Nature Reserves
- Marsh
- Waterfall

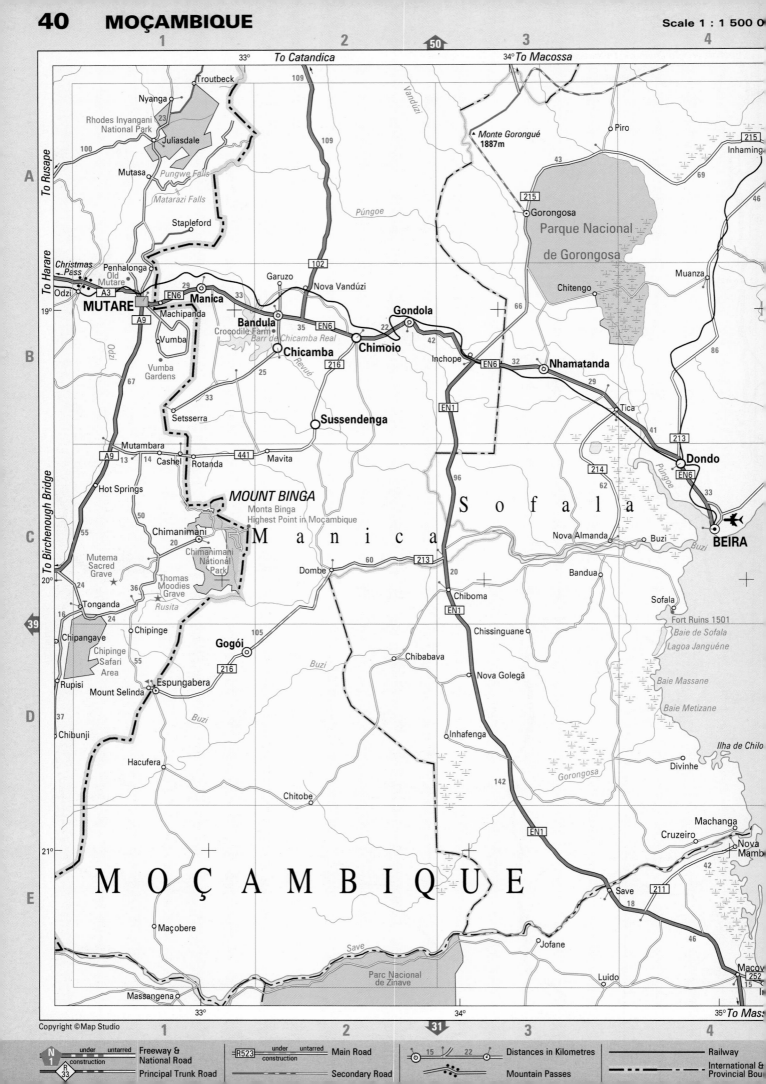

uadala To Lacedornia To Lacedornia 36°
53
nhamitanga
219
213
Marromeu Luabo
R. Mucarau
Micaúne
224

S o f a l a

Chinde

Reserva de Marromeu
Ilha Inhacamba

Nessona
Ilha Timbué

Ilha Micungune
Zambezi Delta

Machesse

Mupa

Moçambique Channel

INDIAN OCEAN

19°

20°

21°

Aerial view of Ponto do Ouro, Moçambique

Ponta don Carlos

Copyright ©Map Studio

Capital or City		Secondary Town		Major Airport		Place of Interest	Toll Route	Game & Nature Reserves
Chief Administrative Town		Other Town		Airfield		Historical Site	Toll Plaza	Marsh
Major Town		Settlement		Accommodation		Border Control	Major Spot Height	Waterfall

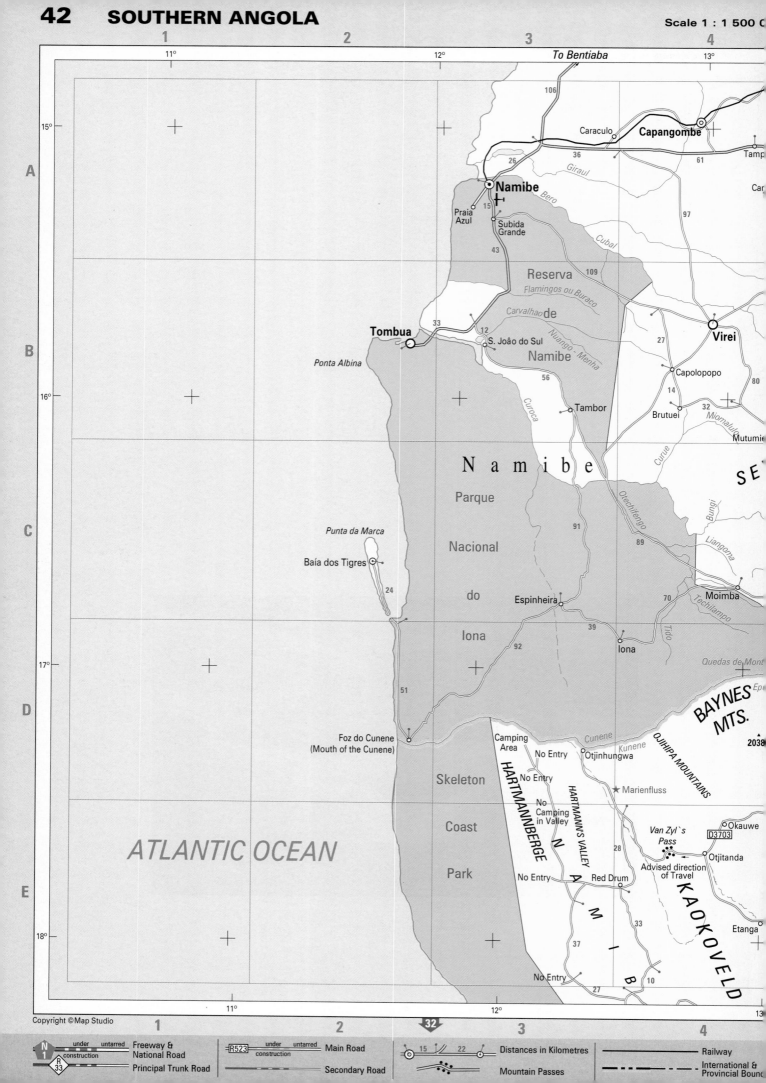

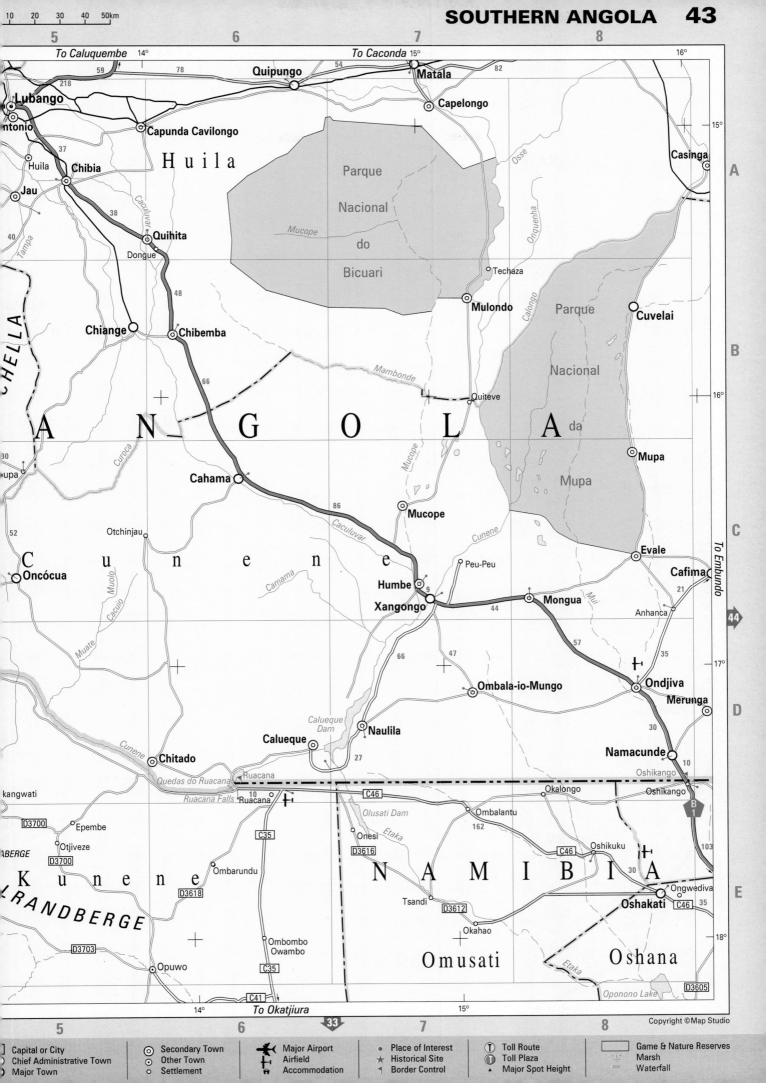

10 20 30 40 50km

To Caluquembe 14°
To Caconda 15°

5   6   7   8

59
78
54
82

Quipungo
Matala
218
Capelongo

Lubango
Casinga
15°
ntonio
Capunda Cavilongo

A

37
H u i l a
Huila

Chibia
Parque

Jau
Nacional

38
do

Quihita
Bicuari
40
Dongue

Trampa
Caculuvar
Mucope

48
Techaza

Mulondo
Parque
Cuvelai

Chiange
Chibemba
Nacional

B

CHELLA

66
Quiteve
da

A N G O L A
16°

Curoca
Mupa
Mupa

Cahama
Mucope
Evale

0
86
Peu-Peu
Cafima

pa
C u n e n e
Caculuvar
Mucope

Otchinjau
Camama
Cunene

C

52
Oncócua
Humbe
9
21

Xangongo
Mongua
Anhanca

Muolo
44
57

Caculo
Muate
66
47
35

Ombala-io-Mungo
Ondjiva
17°
Merunga

D

Calueque
Dam
Naulila
30

Calueque
Namacunde

Chitado
27
10
Oshikango

Cunene
Okalongo

Quedas do Ruacana
Ruacana
Oshikango

kangwati
Ruacana Falls
10
Ruacana
C46
Ombalantu
103

D3700
Epembe
C35
Olusati Dam
162
Oshikuku
C46

Otjiveze
Onesi
30

ABERGE
D3700
D3616
30

K u n e n e
N A M I B I A

D3618
Ombarundu

E

LRANDBERGE
Tsandi
D3612
Ongwediva
Oshakati
C46
35

D3703
Okahao
18°

Ombombo
Owambo

Opuwo
Omusati
Oshana

C35
Oponono Lake
D3605

C41
To Okatjiura

14°
15°

5   6   7   8

33

Copyright ©Map Studio

Legend		
Capital or City	Secondary Town	Major Airport
Chief Administrative Town	Other Town	Airfield
Major Town	Settlement	Accommodation
Place of Interest	Toll Route	Game & Nature Reserves
Historical Site	Toll Plaza	Marsh
Border Control	Major Spot Height	Waterfall

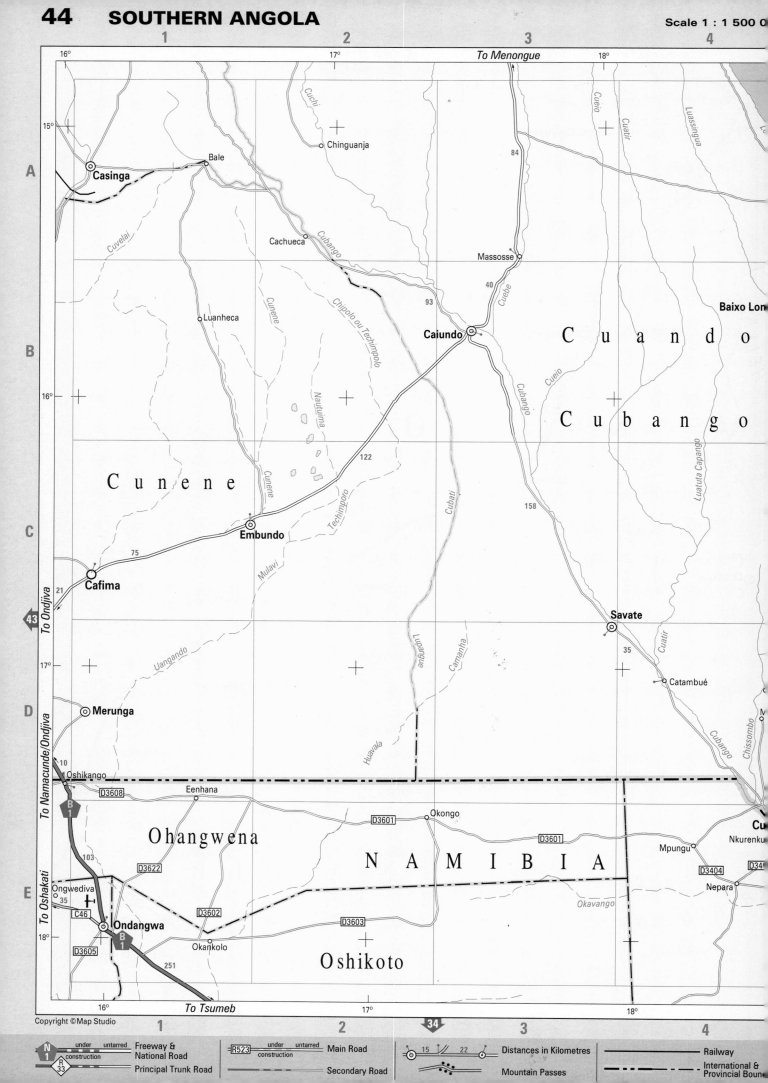

To Menongue

16°   17°   18°

15°

A

Casinga
Bale
Chinguanja

Cuchi
Cuvelai
Cubango
Cachueca
Massosse
84

Cueio
Cuatir
Luassingua

B

16°

Luanheca
Chipolo ou Techimpolo
Caiundo
93
40
Cuebe

C u a n d o

Baixo Lon

Cunene
Cunene
Nautuima
Cubango
Cueio

C u b a n g o

122

Luatuta Capango

C

Embundo
75
Techimpolo
Cubati
158

C u n e n e

Mulavi

Cafima
21

To Ondjiva
43

Savate
35
Cuatir

17°

Uangando
Lupangue
Camanha
Catambué

D

Merunga

Huavala
Cubango
Chissombo
M

To Namacunde/Ondjiva
10
Oshikango

D3608
Eenhana
B 1

O h a n g w e n a
Okongo
D3601

D3601
Cu
Nkurenku

103
D3622

N A M I B I A
Mpungu
D3404
D34

E

Ongwediva
35
C46
D3602
Okavango
Nepara

To Oshakati
Ondangwa
B 1
D3603

18°
D3605
Okankolo
251

O s h i k o t o

16°   To Tsumeb   17°   18°

Copyright ©Map Studio

1   2   **34**   3   4

N 1 under construction / untarred Freeway & National Road
R 33 Principal Trunk Road

R523 under construction / untarred Main Road
Secondary Road

15 22 Distances in Kilometres
Mountain Passes

Railway
International & Provincial Boune

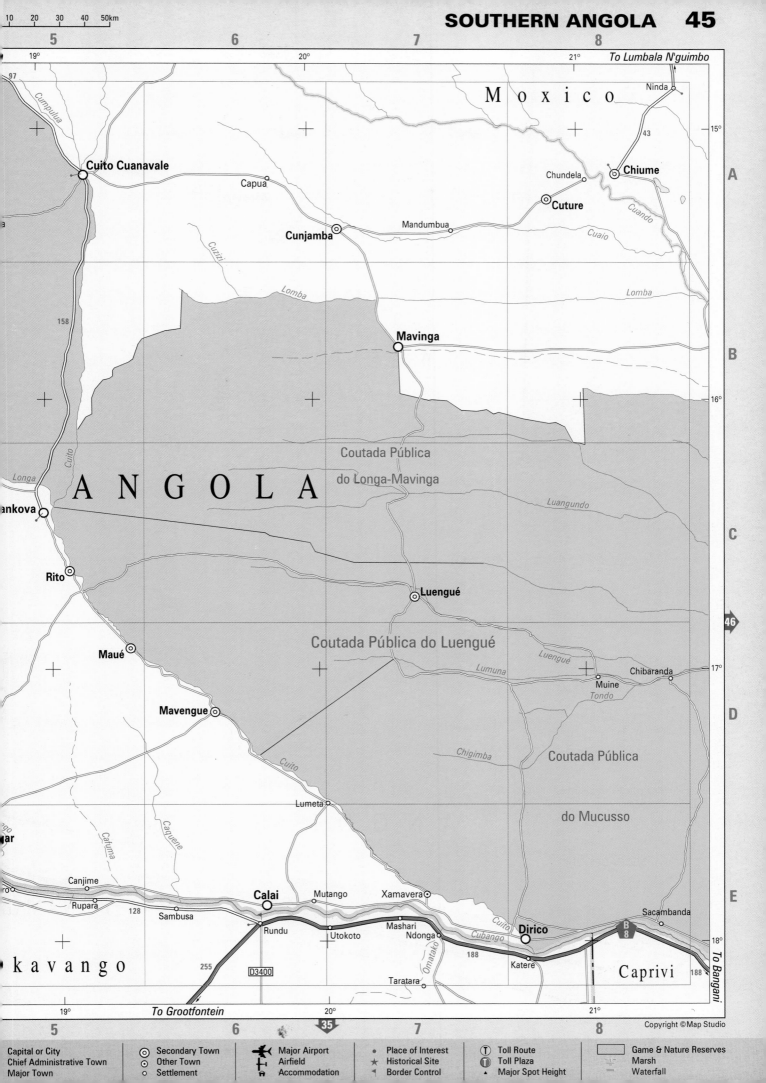

10 20 30 40 50km

5 **6** **7** **8**

19° 20° 21° *To Lumbala N'guimbo*

M o x i c o

97

Ninda

Cumpulua

15°

Cuito Cuanavale Chundela **Chiume** A

Capua 43

Cuture

Cuzizi Mandumbua Cuando

Cunjamba Cuaio

Lomba

Lomba

158

Mavinga B

16°

Cuito

Coutada Pública

Longa

do Longa-Mavinga

A N G O L A Luangundo

ankova C

Rito

Luengué 46

Coutada Pública do Luengué

Lumuna Luengué

Maué Chibaranda 17°

Muine

Tondo

Mavengue Coutada Pública D

Cuito Chigimba

do Mucusso

Lumeta

Caquene

ago Canjime

Caetuma

Calai Mutango Xamavera Sacambanda E

ar Rupara 128 Cuito

Sambusa Rundu Mashari **Dirico** B8 18°

Utokoto Ndonga Cubango

D3400 Katere Caprivi 188

k a v a n g o 255 Omataku 188

Taratara *To Bangani*

To Grootfontein

5 **6** 35 **7** **8**

Copyright ©Map Studio

Capital or City | Secondary Town | Major Airport | Place of Interest | Toll Route | Game & Nature Reserves
Chief Administrative Town | Other Town | Airfield | Historical Site | Toll Plaza | Marsh
Major Town | Settlement | Accommodation | Border Control | Major Spot Height | Waterfall

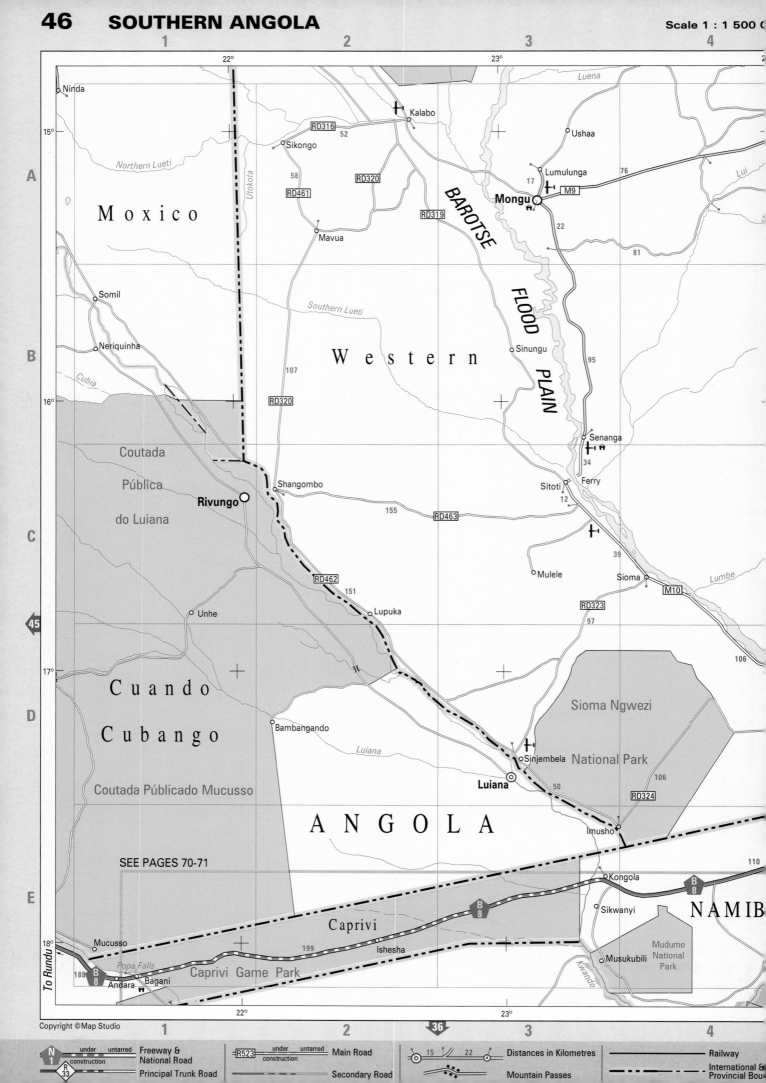

Ninda

15°

RD316
52
Kalabo
Sikongo

Ushaa

A
58
RD320
Lumulunga
17
76
RD461
Mongu
M9

RD319
22
81

M o x i c o

Mavua

Northern Lueti

Utokota

B A R O T S E

Somil

Southern Lueti

Sinungu

F L O O D

B
107
RD320
95

W e s t e r n

16°

Cubia
Neriquinha

Senanga
34

P L A I N

Coutada
Shangombo
Sitoti
Ferry
12

Pública
Rivungo
155
RD463

do Luiana
Mulele
39

C
RD462
Sioma
M10
Lumbe
151
RD323

Unhe
Lupuka
97

45
17°

C u a n d o
106

Bambangando
Sioma Ngwezi

D
Luiana
National Park

C u b a n g o
Sinjembela
106
RD324
50

Coutada Pública do Mucusso
Luiana

A N G O L A
Imusho

SEE PAGES 70-71
110

Kongola
B
8

E
Sikwanyi
NAMIB

Caprivi
B
8

18°
Mucusso
199
Ishesha
Musukubili
Mudumo
National
Park

To Rundu
Popa Falls
Caprivi Game Park
Kwando

188
B
8
Bagani
Andara

22°
23°

Copyright ©Map Studio

36

N 1	under untarred construction	Freeway & National Road	R523	under untarred construction	Main Road
R 33		Principal Trunk Road			Secondary Road

15 ↑ 22 Distances in Kilometres
Mountain Passes

Railway
International & Provincial Bou

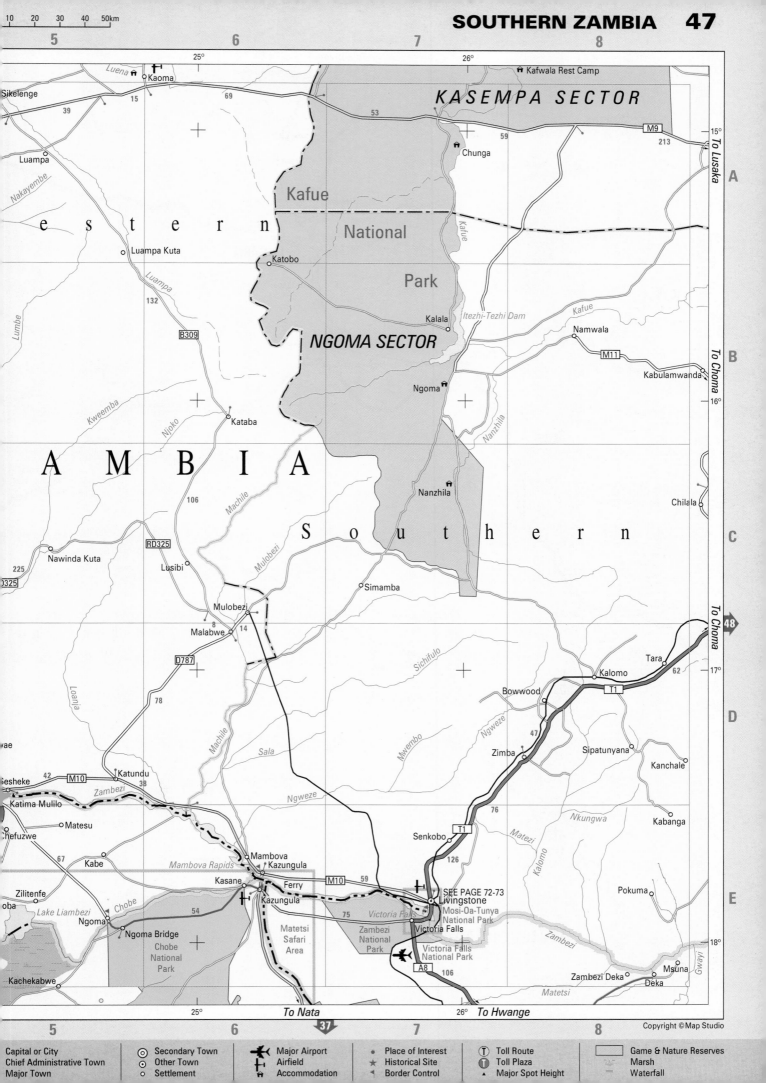

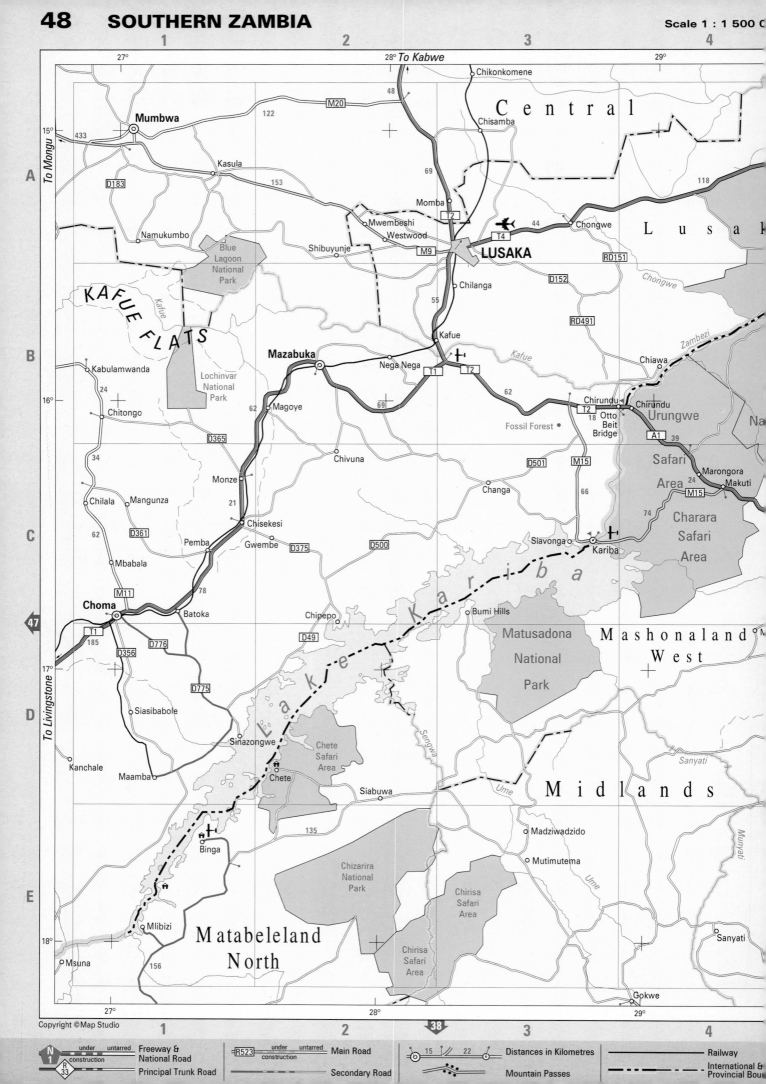

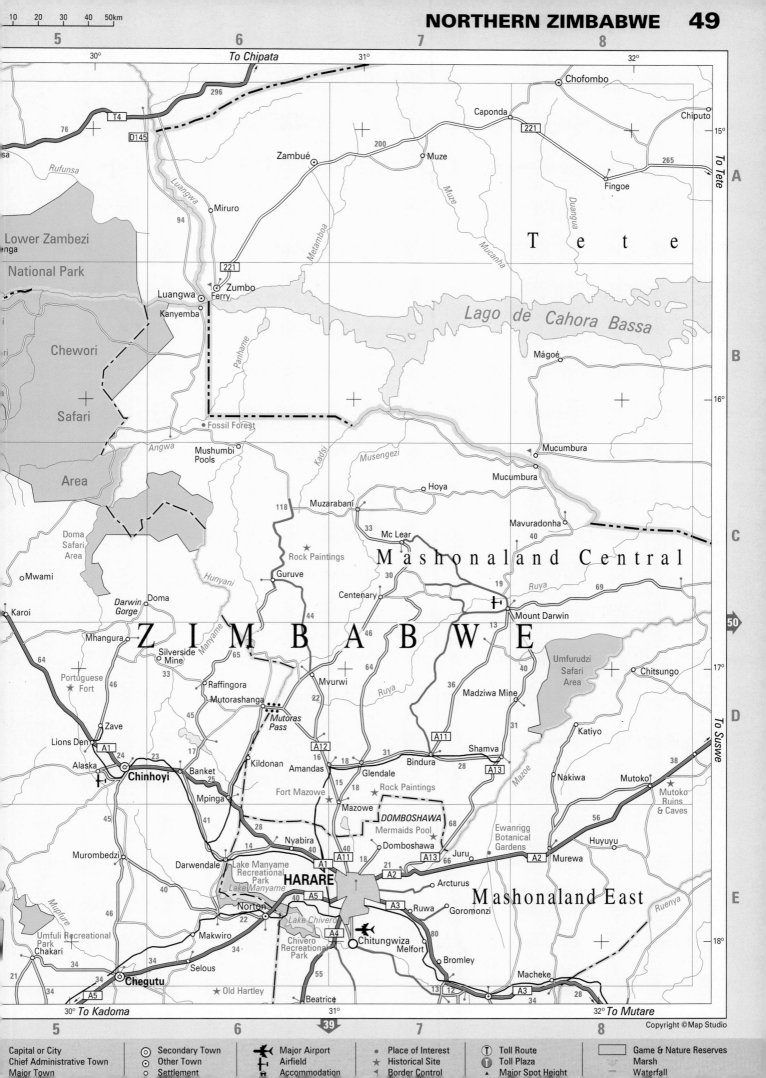

Scale: 10 20 30 40 50km

To Chipata

To Tete

To Suswe

To Kadoma

To Mutare

T e t e

Lower Zambezi National Park

Chewori Safari Area

Doma Safari Area

Lago de Cahora Bassa

M a s h o n a l a n d   C e n t r a l

Z I M B A B W E

Mashonaland East

Umfurudzi Safari Area

Umfuli Recreational Park

Lake Manyame Recreational Park

Chivero Recreational Park

Mutoko Ruins & Caves

Ewanrigg Botanical Gardens

Portuguese Fort

HARARE

Chofombo
Caponda
Chiputo
Fingoe
Zambué
Muze
Miruro
Mágoé
Mucumbura
Mucumbura
Hoya
Mc Lear
Mavuradonha
Chitsungo
Muzarabani
Guruve
Centenary
Mount Darwin
Rock Paintings
Mushumbi Pools
Fossil Forest
Luangwa
Ferry
Zumbo
Kanyemba
Mwami
Karoi
Darwin Gorge
Doma
Mhangura
Silverside Mine
Raffingora
Mvurwi
Madziwa Mine
Shamva
Katiyo
Nakiwa
Mutoko
Mutorashanga
Mutoras Pass
Zave
Lions Den
Alaska
Chinhoyi
Banket
Kildonan
Amandas
Glendale
Bindura
Mpinga
Fort Mazowe
Rock Paintings
Mazowe
Juru
Murewa
Huyuyu
Murombedzi
Darwendale
Nyabira
DOMBOSHAWA
Mermaids Pool
Domboshawa
Arcturus
Norton
Ruwa
Goromonzi
Makwiro
Chitungwiza
Melfort
Bromley
Macheke
Chakari
Selous
Old Hartley
Beatrice
Chegutu

Rufunsa
Luangwa
Metamboa
Muze
Duangua
Mucanha
Panhame
Kadsi
Angwa
Musengezi
Hunyani
Manyame
Ruya
Ruya
Mazoe
Mupfure
Ruenya
Lake Manyame
Lake Chivero

T4
D145
221
221
296
200
265
76
94
118
33
30
46
44
19
69
13
40
40
31
38
64
65
33
22
64
36
31
46
56
45
17
16
18
31
28
41
14
40
40
18
21
66
68
80
46
40
22
34
34
55
45
24
23
25
A1
A12
A11
A13
A11
A1
A2
A2
A13
A3
A4
A5
A5
A3
13
12
34
28
21
34
34

Capital or City
Chief Administrative Town
Major Town
Secondary Town
Other Town
Settlement
Major Airport
Airfield
Accommodation
Place of Interest
Historical Site
Border Control
Toll Route
Toll Plaza
Major Spot Height
Game & Nature Reserves
Marsh
Waterfall

Scale 1 : 1 500 0

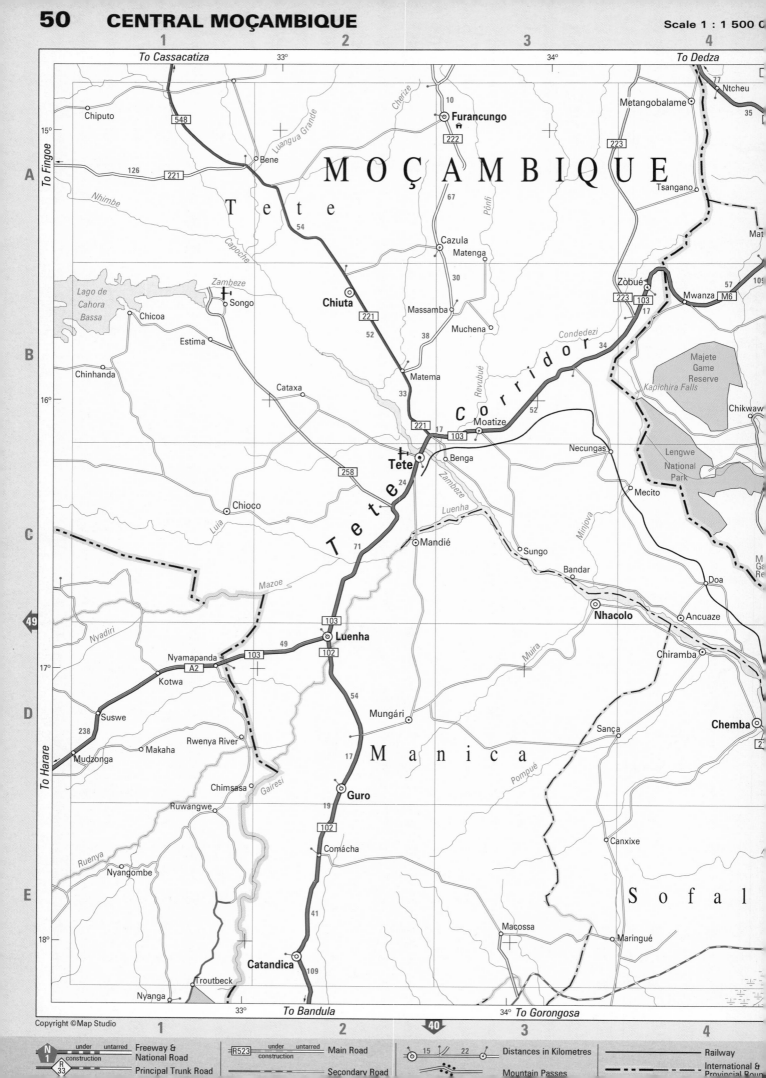

MOÇAMBIQUE

Tete

Manica

Sofal

Copyright ©Map Studio

To Cassacatiza · To Fingoe · To Dedza · To Harare · To Bandula · To Gorongosa

Chiputo · Bene · Chipoco · Songo · Chicoa · Estima · Chinhanda · Cataxa · Chiuta · Matema · Cazula · Matenga · Massamba · Muchena · Furancungo · Tsangano · Metangobalame · Ntcheu · Zòbué · Mwanza · Moatize · Tete · Benga · Necungas · Mecito · Chikwaw · Mandié · Sungo · Bandar · Doa · Nhacolo · Ancuaze · Chiramba · Chioco · Luenha · Nyamapanda · Kotwa · Mungári · Sança · Chemba · Suswe · Makaha · Rwenya River · Chimsasa · Ruwangwe · Guro · Comácha · Canxixe · Nyangombe · Macossa · Maringué · Catandica · Troutbeck · Nyanga · Mudzonga

Lago de Cahora Bassa · Majete Game Reserve · Lengwe National Park · Kapichira Falls

Zambeze · Luangua Grande · Cherize · Pônfi · Capoche · Nhimbe · Revubué · Condedezi · Luenha · Zambeze · Luia · Mazoe · Nyadiri · Minjova · Muira · Gairesi · Pompué · Ruenya

Corridor

under construction	untarred	Freeway & National Road
		Principal Trunk Road
R523 under construction	untarred	Main Road
		Secondary Road
15 / 22		Distances in Kilometres
		Mountain Passes
		Railway
		International & Provincial Bou

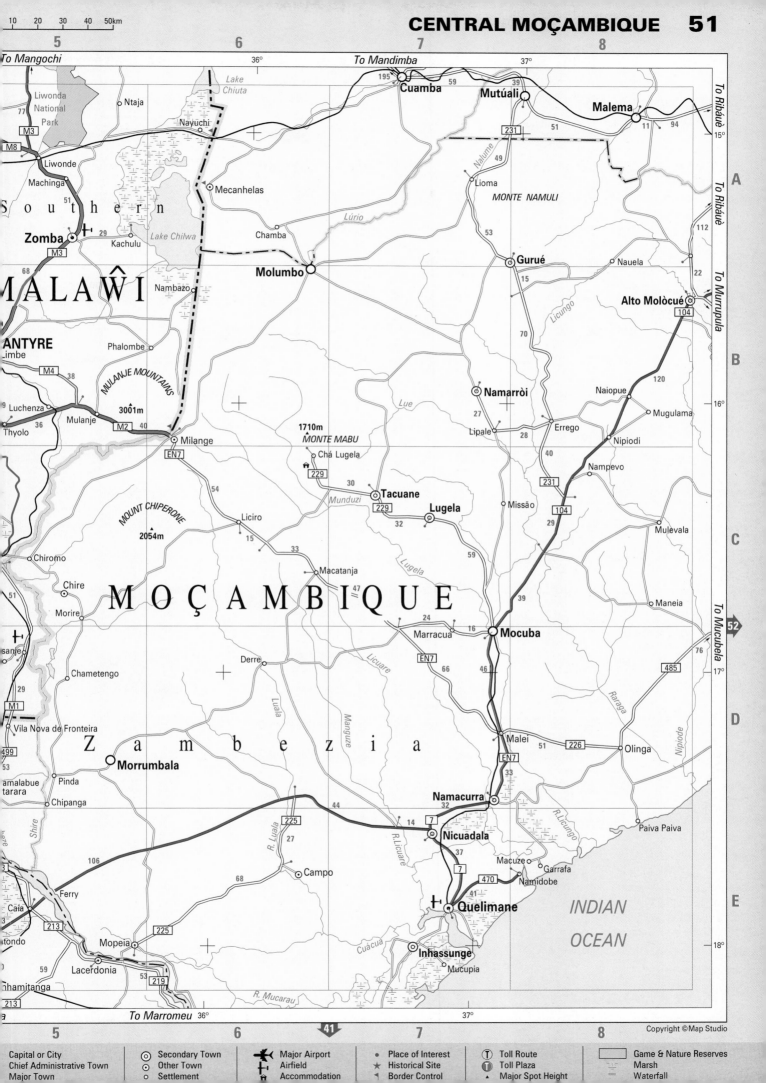

Scale
10 20 30 40 50km

5 · **6** · **7** · **8**

To Mangochi
To Mandimba
To Ribáuè
To Ribáuè
To Murrupula

A

Liwonda National Park
M3
M8
Ntaja
Nayuchi
Lake Chiuta
195
Cuamba
59
Mutúali
39
231
Malema
51
11
94
15°
Mecanhelas
Lúrio
49
Lioma
MONTE NAMULI
77
Liwonde
Machinga
51
Southern
Chamba
53
Gurué
15
Nauela
22
112

B

Zomba
M3
29
Kachulu
Lake Chilwa
Molumbo
Alto Molòcué
104
MALAŴI
Nambazo
Licungo
70
ANTYRE
imbe
M4
Phalombe
38
MULANJE MOUNTAINS
3001m
Namarròi
27
Naiopue
120
Mugulama
16°
9 Luchenza
Mulanje
M2 40
Lue
Lipale
28
Errego
Nipiodi
Thyolo
36
Milange
EN7
Lugela
40
Nampevo
231

C

1710m
MONTE MABU
Chá Lugela
229
30
Tacuane
229
Lugela
32
104
29
Mulevala
Mount Chiperone
2054m
Liciro
15
Munduzi
Missão
Chiromo
33
59
Maneia
To Mucubela
52
Morire
Macatanja
47
M O Ç A M B I Q U E
24
39

D

51
Derre
Marracua
16
Mocuba
76
485
Chametengo
Licuare
EN7
66
46
17°
M1
Luala
Manguze
Malei
226
Olinga
sanje
Vila Nova de Fronteira
499
53
Z a m b e z i a
Morrumbala
Raraga
Nipiode
amalabue
tarara
Pinda
51
EN7
Chipanga
33
Namacurra
32

E

Shire
225
44
14
7
Nicuadala
27
37
106
Campo
68
470
Macuze
Garrafa
Namidobe
Ferry
41
Caia
213
Quelimane
INDIAN
225
Cuácua
OCEAN
Mopeia
18°
59
Lacerdonia
53
219
Mucupia
Inhassunge
hamitanga
213

To Marromeu 36°
To Mandimba
37°

41

5 · **6** · **7** · **8**

Copyright ©Map Studio

Legend
Capital or City	◉ Secondary Town	✈ Major Airport	• Place of Interest	Ⓣ Toll Route	▢ Game & Nature Reserves
Chief Administrative Town	◎ Other Town	Airfield	★ Historical Site	Ⓣ Toll Plaza	Marsh
Major Town	◦ Settlement	Accommodation	▼ Border Control	▲ Major Spot Height	Waterfall

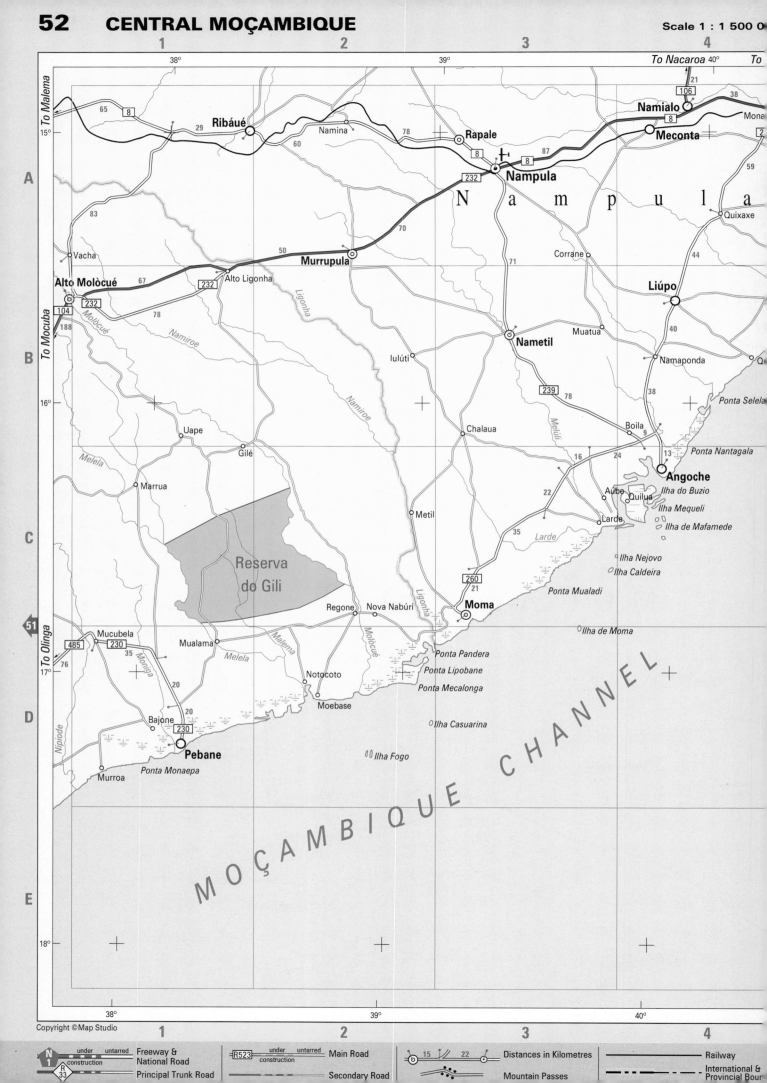

To Nacaroa 40° To

To Malema

65 8

29 Ribáué

Namina

78

Rapale

8

87

Namialo

8

Meconta

Mona

21

106

38

38

To Mocuba

83

Vacha

50 Murrupula

70

N a m p u l a

Quixaxe

59

Alto Molòcué

67 Alto Ligonha

232

78

Ligonha

71

Corrane

44

Liúpo

104

232

188

Molòcué

Namiroe

Namiroe

Iulúti

Nametil

Muatua

40

Namaponda

Q

239 78

38

Ponta Selela

Melela

Uape

Gilé

Chalaua

Meluli

Boila

9

13

Ponta Nantagala

Marrua

16

24

Angoche

Ilha do Buzio

Reserva
do Gili

22

Aúbe Quilua

Ilha Mequeli

Metil

Larde

35 Larde

Ilha de Mafamede

Ilha Nejovo

Ilha Caldeira

Regone Nova Nabúri

260
21

Moma

Ponta Mualadi

To Olinga

Mucubela

485 230

Moniga 35

Mualama

Malema

Melela

Ligonha

Molòcué

Ilha de Moma

Ponta Pandera

Ponta Lipobane

76

20

Notocoto

Ponta Mecalonga

20

Bajone

230

Moebase

Ilha Casuarina

Nipiode

Pebane

Ilha Fogo

Ponta Monaepa

Murroa

M O Ç A M B I Q U E   C H A N N E L

Copyright ©Map Studio

N
1

R
33

under untarred
construction

Freeway &
National Road

Principal Trunk Road

R523 under untarred
construction

Main Road

Secondary Road

15 22

Distances in Kilometres

Mountain Passes

Railway

International &
Provincial Bour

5 10 20 30 40 50km

5   6   7   8

41°   42°   43°

Matibane

Baía da Condúcia

21

5   Mossuril

Lumbo   *Ilha de Moçambique*

26   ◎ World Heritage Site

Moçambique

monho

Ponta Bajone

unga

cual

15°

A

INDIAN OCEAN

B

16°

C

17°

D

Moçambique Island

E

18°

41°   42°   43°

5   6   7   8

Copyright ©Map Studio

Capital or City	Secondary Town	Major Airport	Place of Interest	Toll Route	Game & Nature Reserves
Chief Administrative Town	Other Town	Airfield	Historical Site	Toll Plaza	Marsh
Major Town	Settlement	Accommodation	Border Control	Major Spot Height	Waterfall

Scale 1 : 25 500 0

0   200   400   600

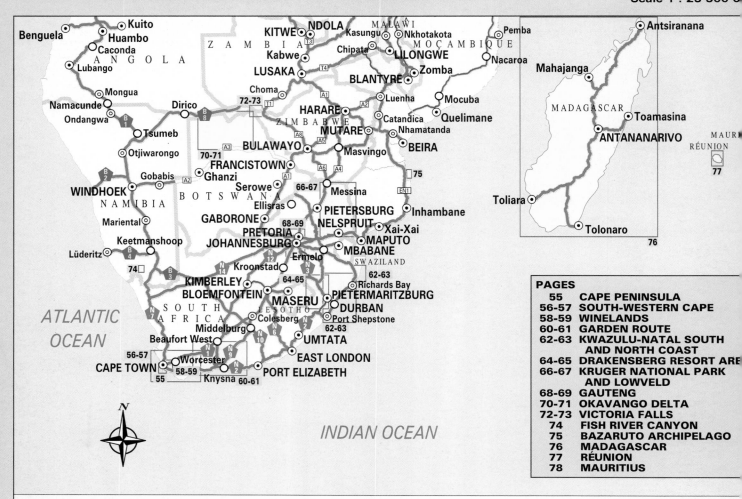

LEGEND TO TOURIST AREA MAPS

tarred / under construction / untarred	Freeway and National Road
	Principal Trunk Road
	Main Road
	Secondary Road
N1 / R33 / R523	Route Numbers
T / T	Toll Route and Toll Plaza
15 22	Distances in Kilometres
	Mountain Passes
	Railway
	International & Provincial Boundary
	National Park and Nature Reserve
	Water Features

▢	Capital or City
⊙	Chief Administrative Town
○	Major Town
◎	Secondary Town
⊙	Other Town
○	Settlement
✈	Major Airport
⊢	Airfield
⌂	Accommodation
•	Place of Interest
★	Historical Site
⌐	Border Control
▲	Major Spot Height
⏄	Marsh
=	Waterfall

Copyright ©Map Studio

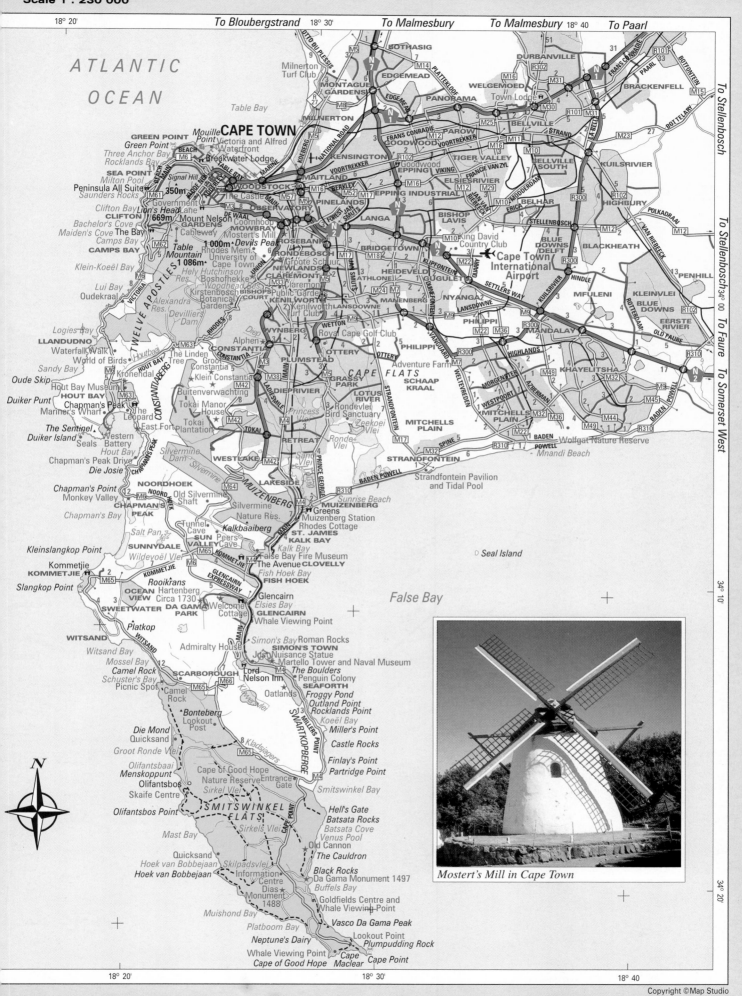

Scale 1 : 230 000

ATLANTIC OCEAN

To Bloubergstrand   To Malmesbury   To Malmesbury   To Paarl

To Stellenbosch
To Stellenbosch
To Faure
To Somerset West

Table Bay

CAPE TOWN

False Bay

Mostert's Mill in Cape Town

N

Copyright ©Map Studio

Capital or City	Secondary Town	Major Airport	Place of Interest	Toll Route	Game & Nature Reserves
Chief Administrative Town	Other Town	Airfield	Historical Site	Toll Plaza	Marsh
Major Town	Settlement	Accommodation	Border Control	Major Spot Height	Waterfall

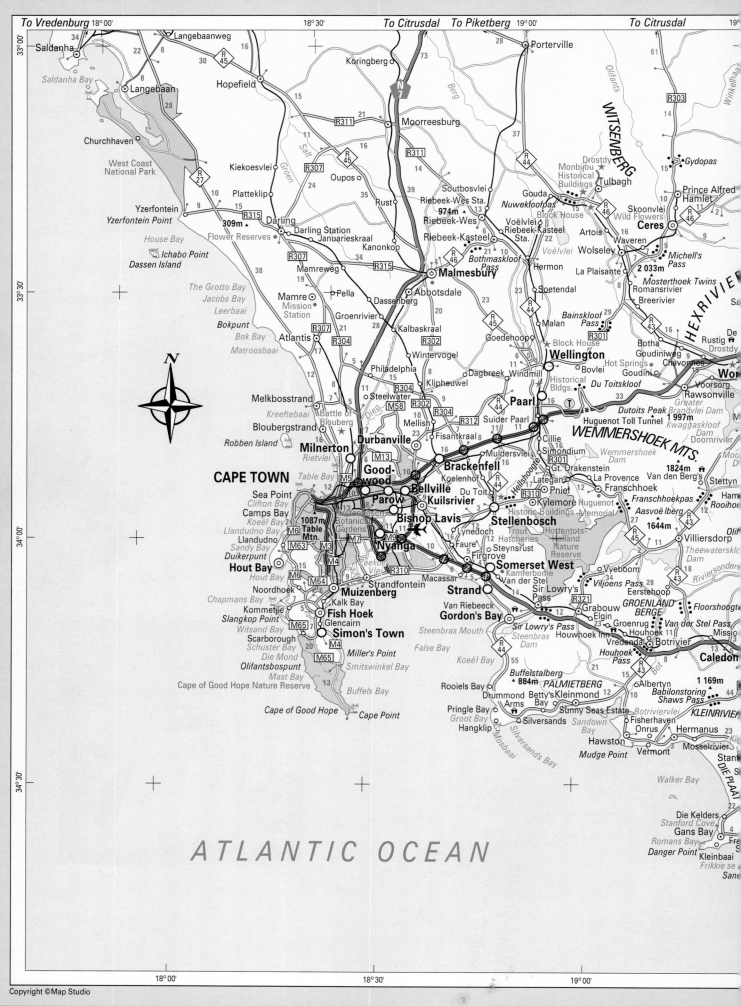

Copyright ©Map Studio

N1 under untarred **Freeway &**
construction **National Road**

R33 **Principal Trunk Road**

R523 under untarred **Main Road**
construction

Secondary Road

○15 ╱ 22 **Distances in Kilometres**

Mountain Passes

Railway

International &
Provincial Rou

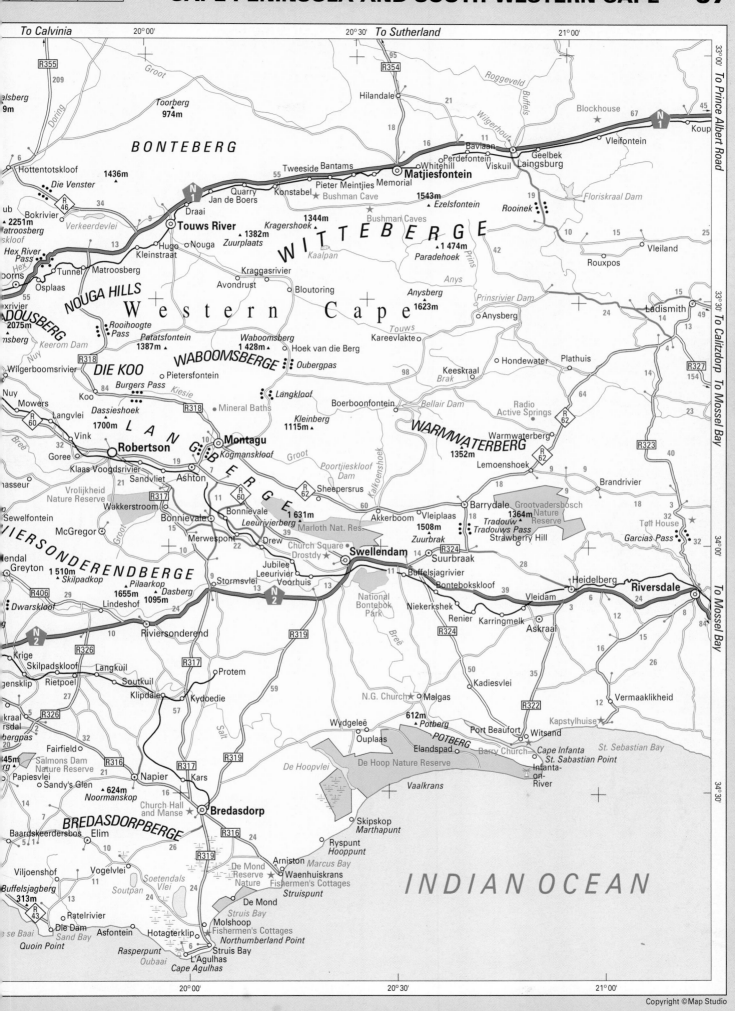

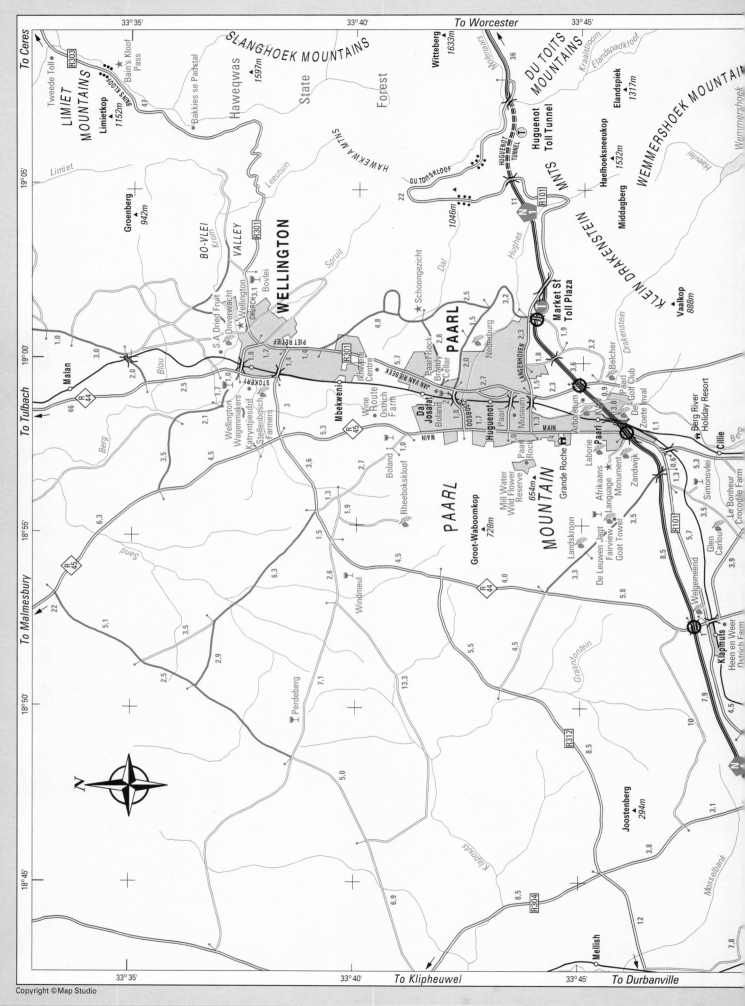

Copyright ©Map Studio

	under construction	untarred	
N1			Freeway & National Road
R33			Principal Trunk Road

	under construction	untarred	
R523			Main Road
			Secondary Road

Distances in Kilometres

Mountain Passes

Railway

International & Provincial Boun

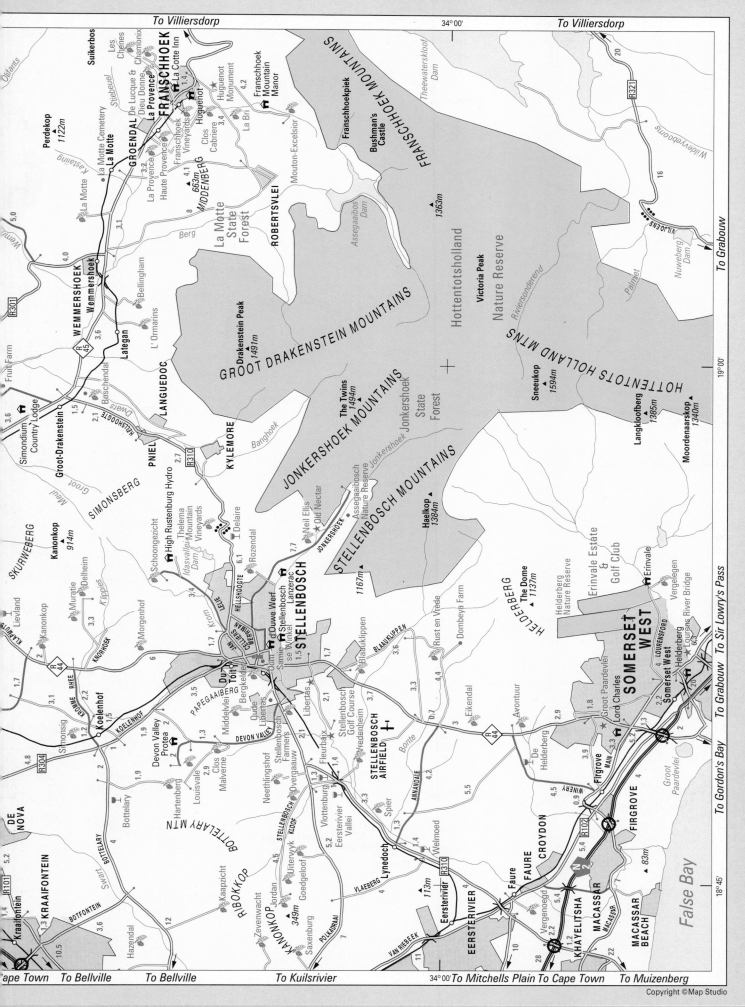

Copyright ©Map Studio

Capital or City	⊙ Secondary Town	✈ Major Airport	• Place of Interest
Chief Administrative Town	◎ Other Town	✈ Airfield	★ Historical Site
Major Town	○ Settlement	⌂ Accommodation	⊟ Border Control

Ⓣ Toll Route	▭ Game & Nature Reserves
Ⓣ Toll Plaza	Wine Co-ops
▲ Major Spot Height	Wineries

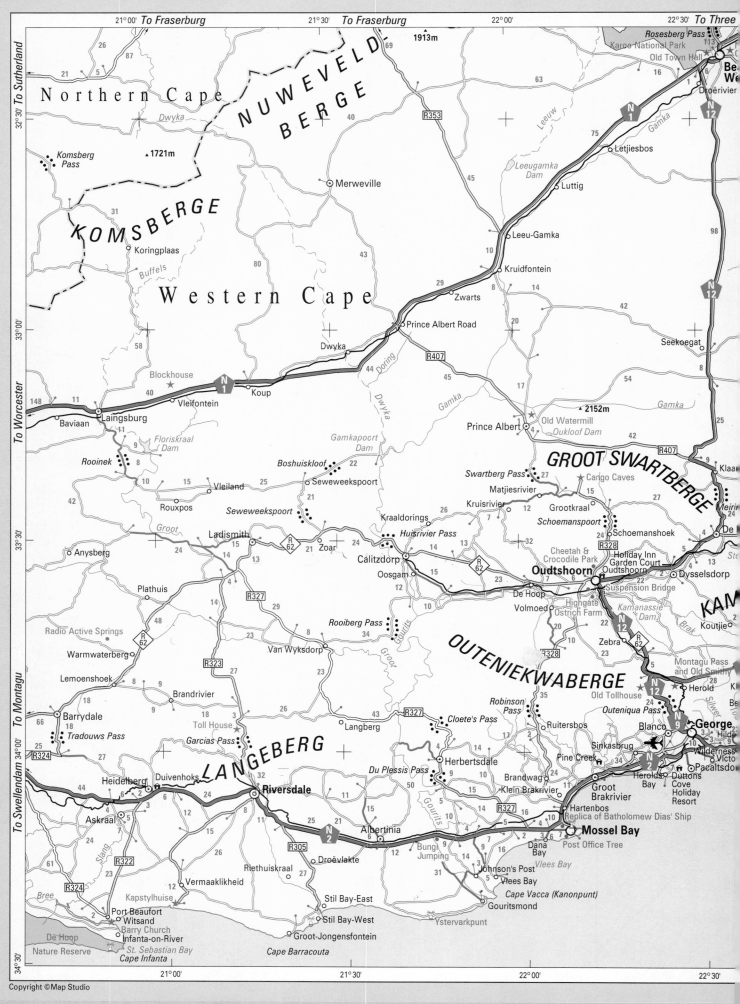

Copyright ©Map Studio

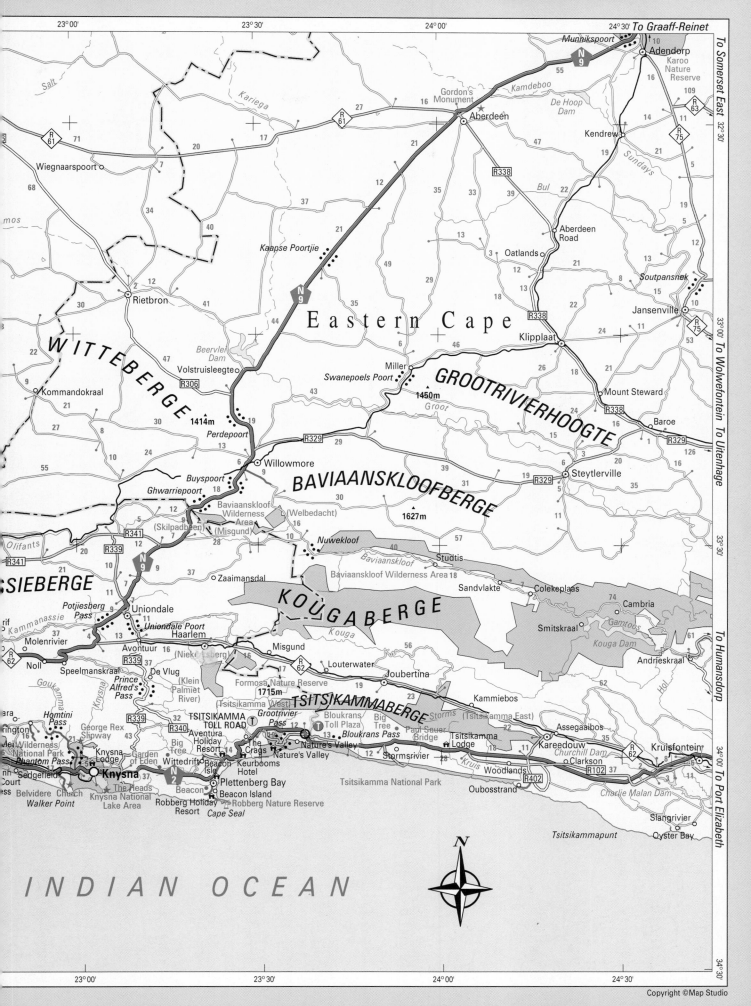

Copyright ©Map Studio

Capital or City	Secondary Town	Major Airport	Place of Interest	Toll Route	Game & Nature Reserves
Chief Administrative Town	Other Town	Airfield	Historical Site	Toll Plaza	Marsh
Major Town	Settlement	Accommodation	Border Control	Major Spot Height	Waterfall

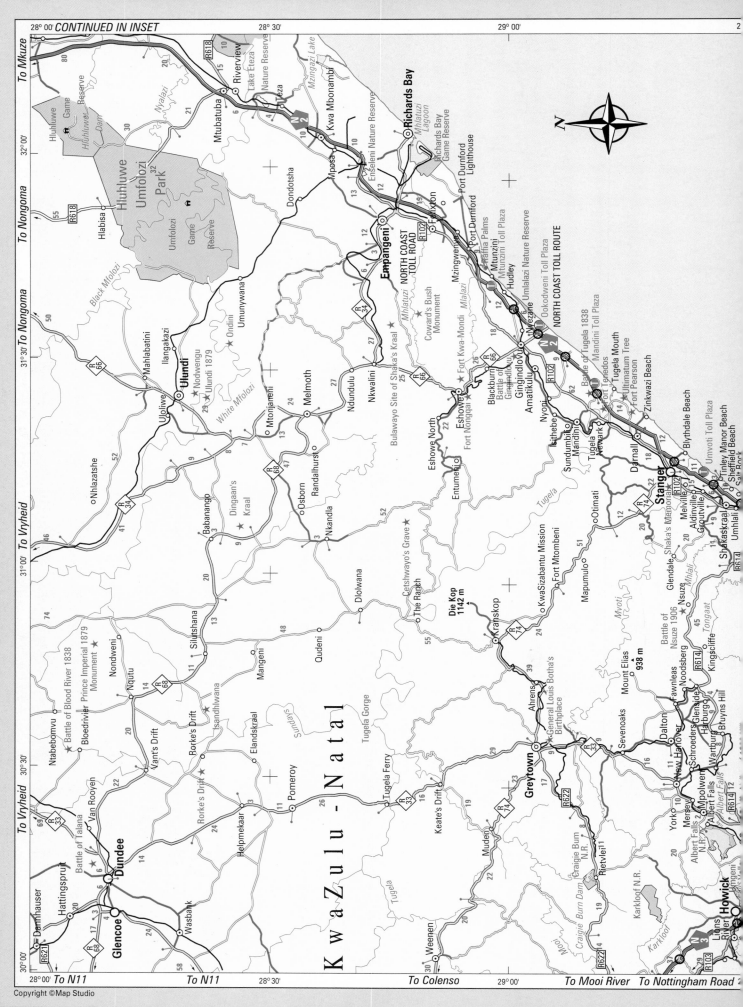

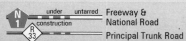

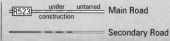

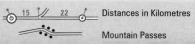

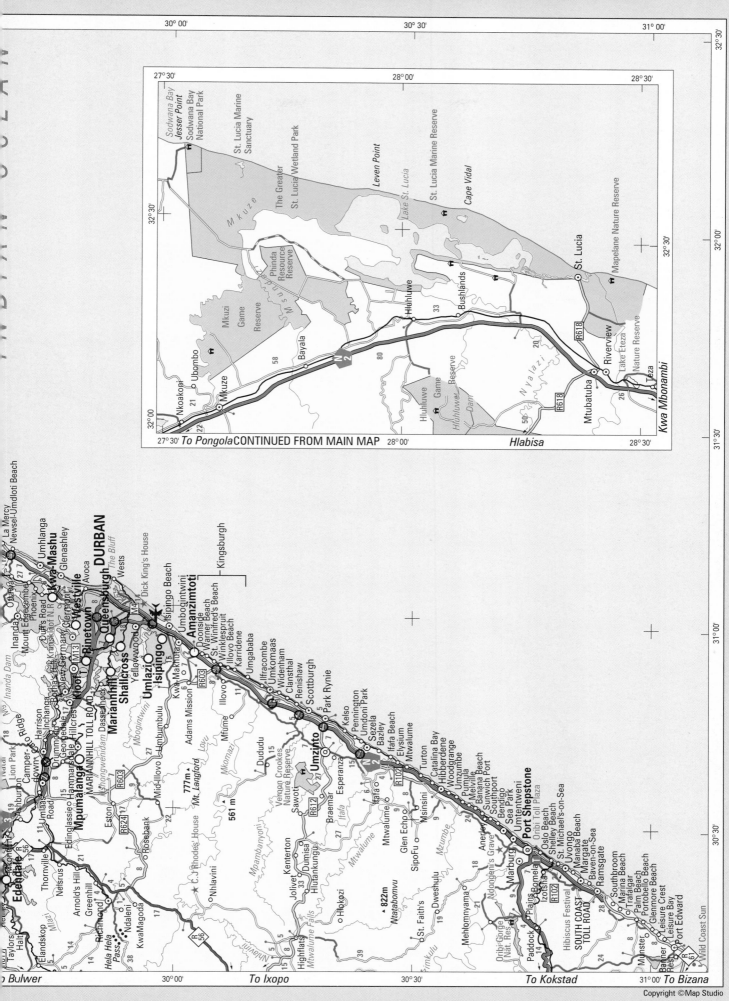

Copyright ©Map Studio

⊚ Capital or City	⊚ Secondary Town	✈ Major Airport	● Place of Interest	Ⓣ Toll Route
Chief Administrative Town	⊙ Other Town	⊢ Airfield	★ Historical Site	Ⓣ Toll Plaza
Major Town	○ Settlement	⌂ Accommodation	◄ Border Control	▲ Major Spot Height

☐ Game & Nature Reserves
Marsh
Waterfall

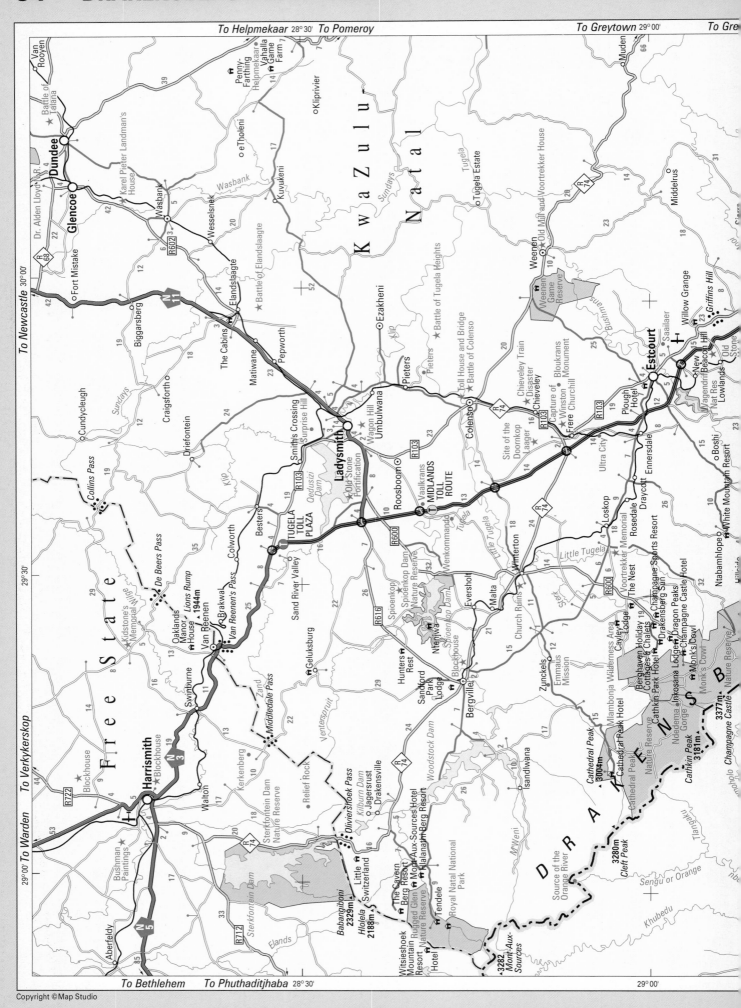

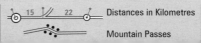

Copyright ©Map Studio

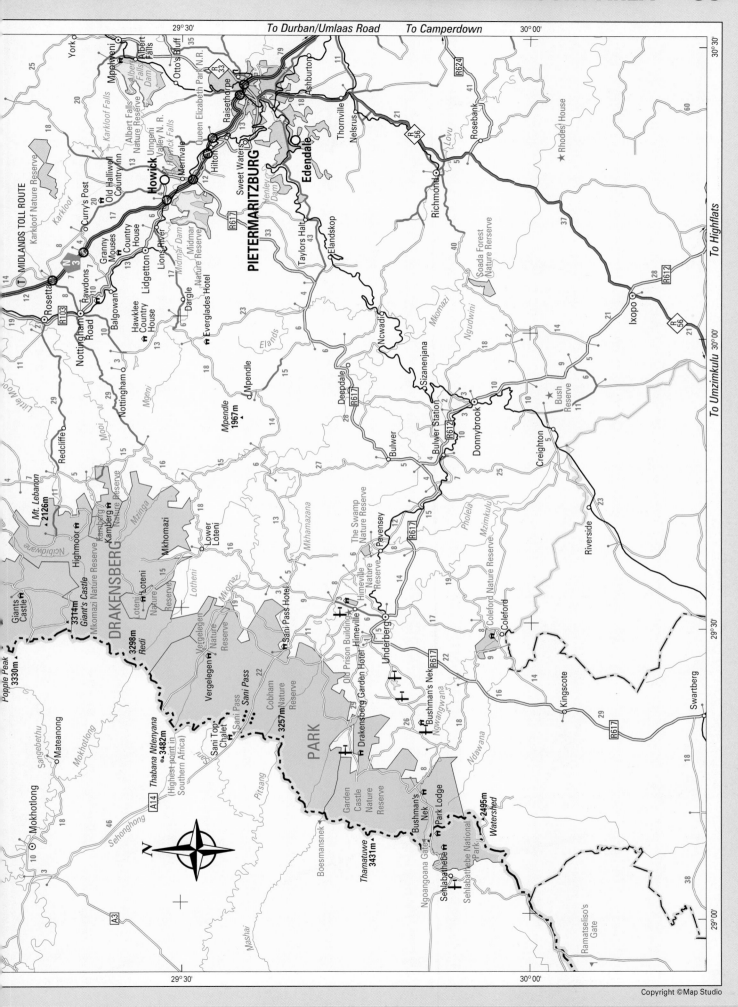

Copyright ©Map Studio

● Capital or City	◉ Secondary Town	✈ Major Airport	● Place of Interest	Ⓣ Toll Route	▢ Game & Nature Reserves
● Chief Administrative Town	⊙ Other Town	Airfield	★ Historical Site	Ⓣ Toll Plaza	Marsh
● Major Town	● Settlement	⌂ Accommodation	✠ Border Control	▲ Major Spot Height	Waterfall

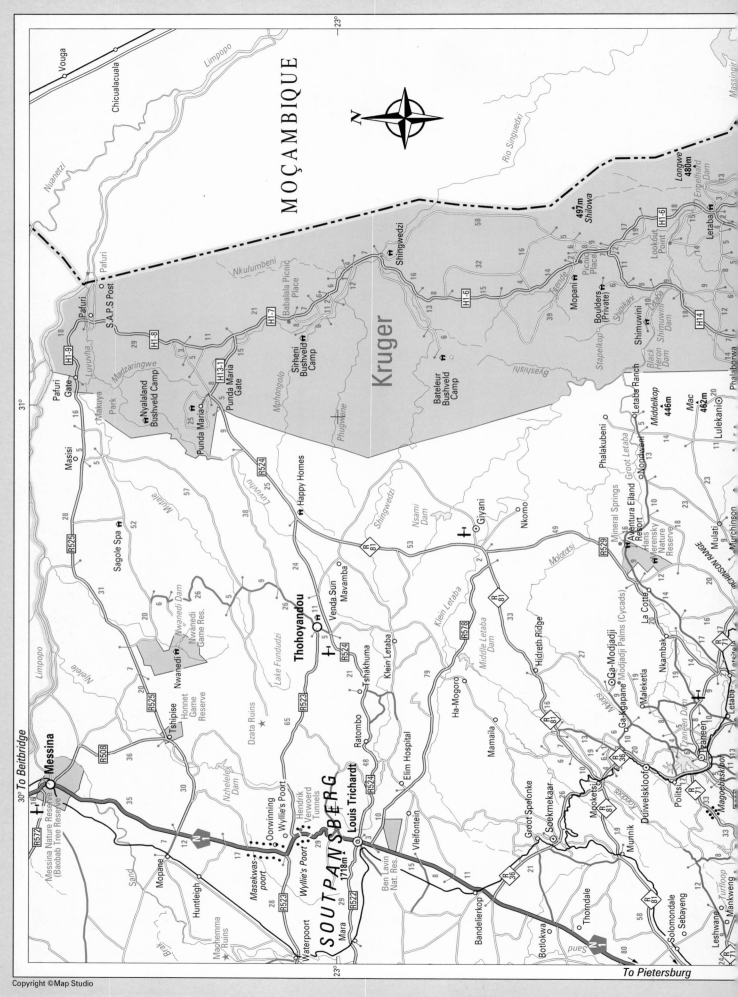

Copyright ©Map Studio

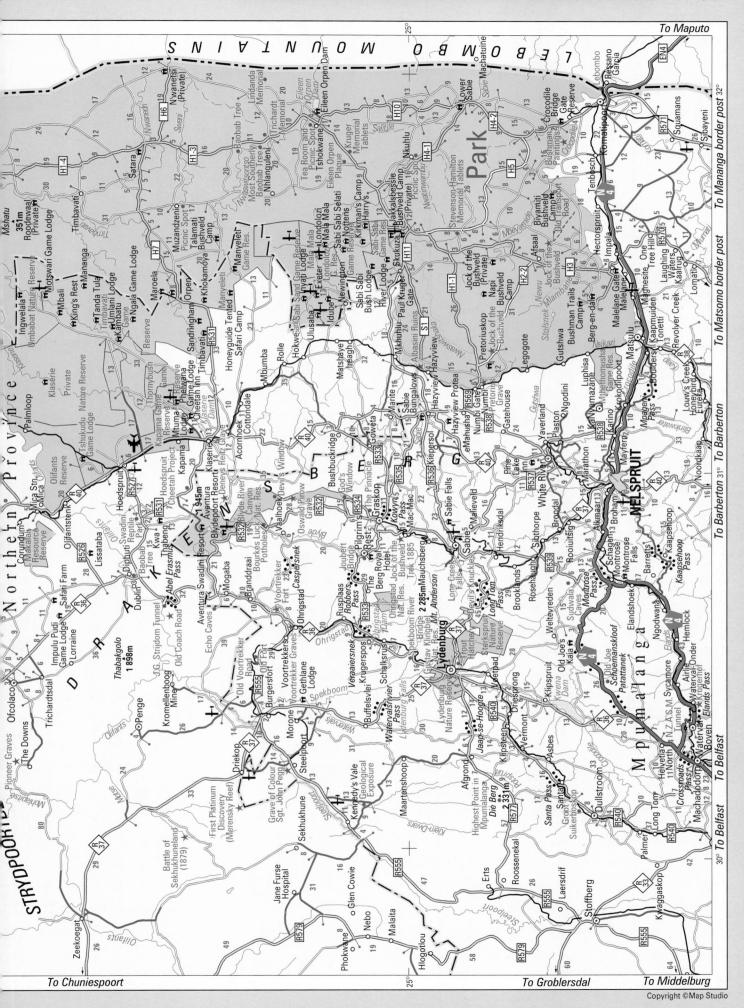

Copyright ©Map Studio

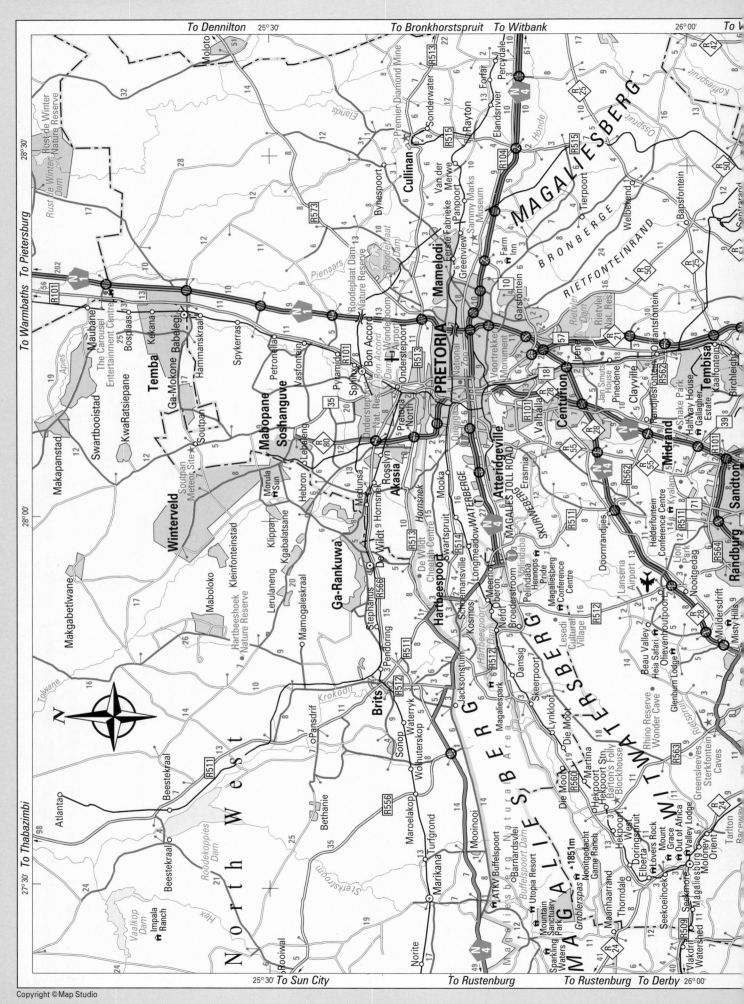

Copyright ©Map Studio

Copyright ©Map Studio

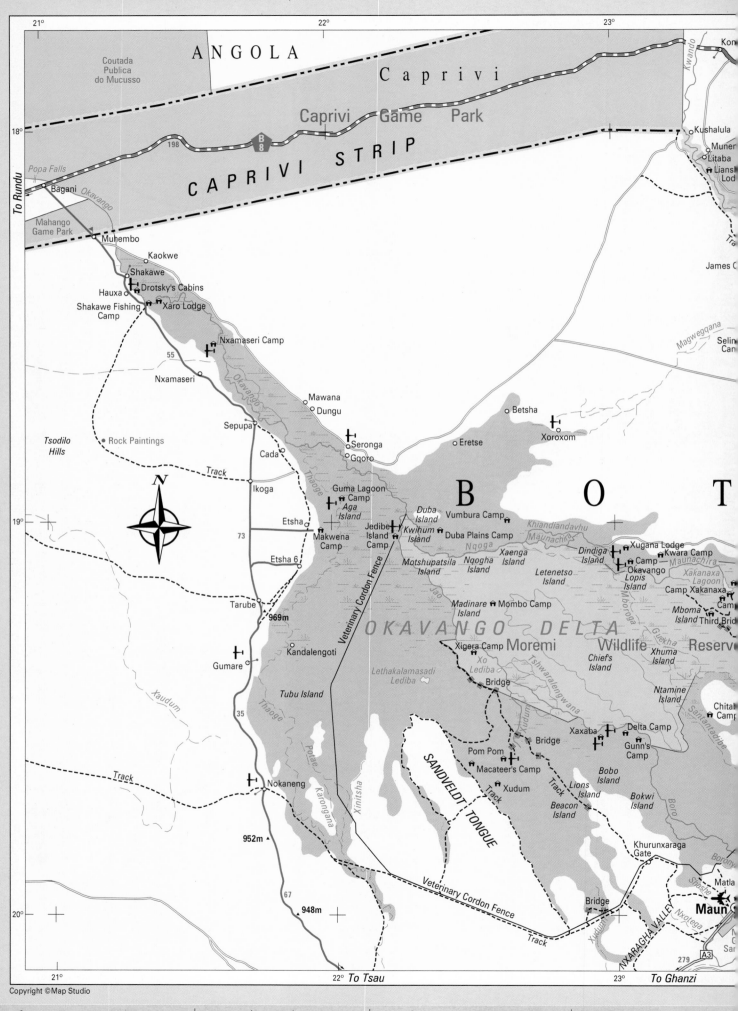

ANGOLA

Coutada
Publica
do Mucusso

Caprivi

Caprivi Game Park

CAPRIVI STRIP

Kwando

Kon

18°

B8
198

Kushalula

Muner
Litaba
Lians
Lod

To Rundu

Popa Falls
Bagani   Okavango

Mahango
Game Park

Muhembo

Kaokwe
Shakawe
Hauxa Drotsky's Cabins
Shakawe Fishing
Camp   Xaro Lodge

James C

Nxamaseri Camp

Magweggana

Seli
Can

55

Nxamaseri

Mawana
Dungu

Betsha
Xoroxom

Sepupa

Cada

Tsodilo
Hills   Rock Paintings

Track

Seronga
Gqoro

Eretse

B   O   T

Ikoga

Guma Lagoon
Camp
Aga
Island

Duba
Island   Vumbura Camp

Khiandiandavhu

Maunachira

Ngoga

19°

73

Etsha

Makwena
Camp

Jedibe
Island
Camp

Kwihum
Island

Duba Plains Camp

Xaenga
Island

Ngoqha
Island

Dindiga
Island

Motshupatsila
Island

Letenetso
Island

Maunachira

Xugana Lodge
Kwara Camp
Camp
Okavango
Lopis
Island

Xakanaxa
Lagoon

Camp Xakanaxa

Cam

Etsha 6

Jao

Madinare
Island   Mombo Camp

Veterinary Cordon Fence

Tarube

969m

OKAVANGO   DELTA

Xigera Camp   Moremi

Mboma
Island   Third Brid

Wildlife   Reserv

Ntamine
Island

Chita
Camp

Kandalengoti

Lethakalamasadi
Lediba

Xo
Lediba

Bridge

Chief's
Island

Xhuma
Island

Gumare

Tubu Island

Thaoge

35

Xaudum

Pelae

Xaxaba   Delta Camp

Bridge

Bobo
Island

Gunn's
Camp

Pom Pom

Macateer's Camp

Xudum

Lions
Island

Beacon
Island

Bokwi
Island

SANDVELDT TONGUE

Track

Khurunxaraga
Gate

Nokaneng

Karongana

Xinitsha

952m

Matla

Bridge

Boro

Shashe

Nxoteg

67

948m

Veterinary Cordon Fence
Track

NXARAGHA VALLEY

279   A3

Maun

Sa

20°

Copyright ©Map Studio

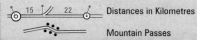

	under	untarred	Freeway & National Road
	construction		Principal Trunk Road

R523	under	untarred	Main Road
	construction		Secondary Road

15   22   Distances in Kilometres

Mountain Passes

Railway

International &
Provincial Boun

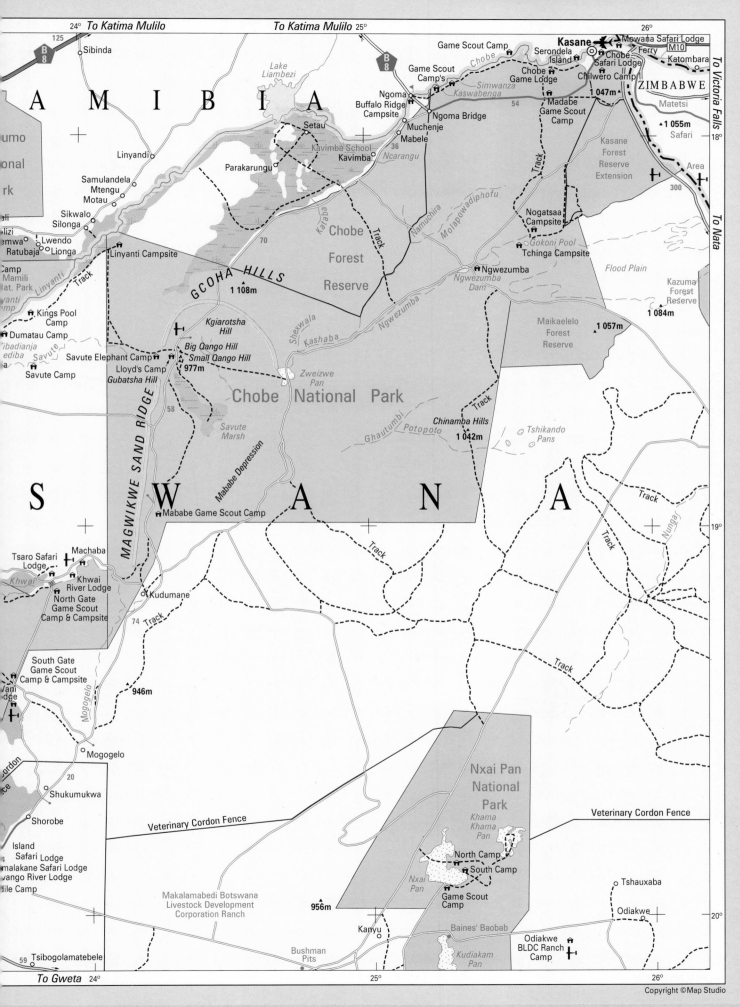

Copyright ©Map Studio

Capital or City	◉ Secondary Town	✈ Major Airport
Chief Administrative Town	◎ Other Town	Airfield
Major Town	○ Settlement	Accommodation

• Place of Interest	Ⓣ Toll Route	Game & Nature Reserves
★ Historical Site	Ⓣ Toll Plaza	Marsh
Border Control	▲ Major Spot Height	Waterfall

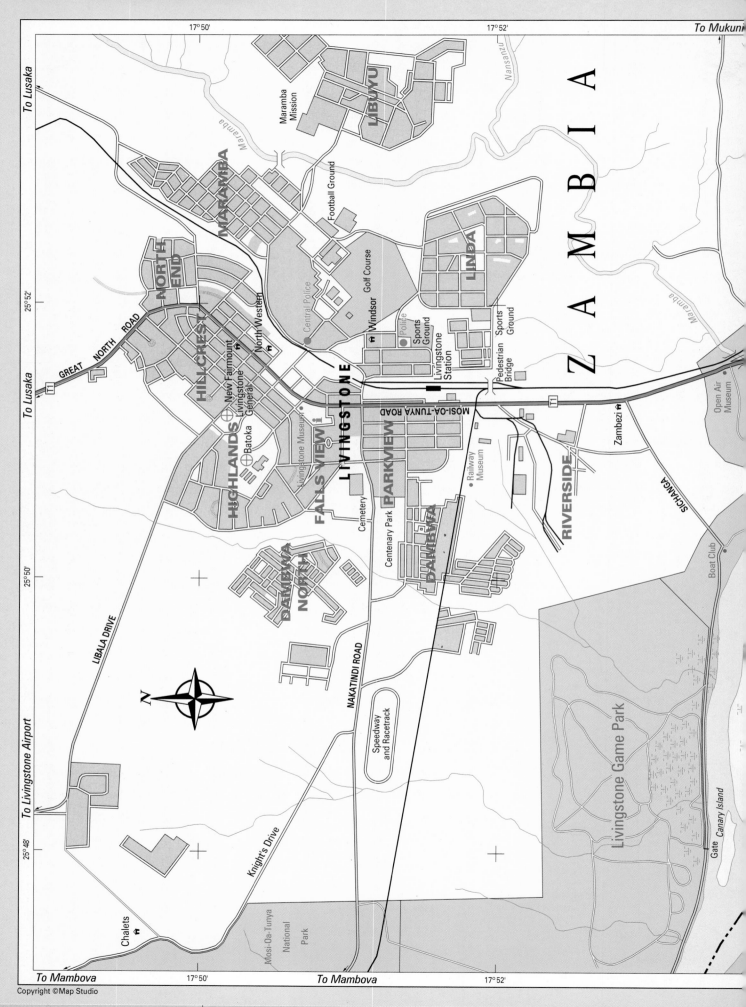

Copyright ©Map Studio

under construction / untarred — **Freeway & National Road** / **Principal Trunk Road**	R523 under construction / untarred — **Main Road** / **Secondary Road**	15 ↑↓ 22 — **Distances in Kilometres** / **Mountain Passes**

— **Railway**

— **International & Provincial Bou**

0.5 1km

17° 56' 17° 58'

25° 52'
25° 50'
25° 48'

Mosi-Oa-Tunya National Park

Manjalide Drive

MOSI-OA-TUNYA ROAD

Lookout Tree (Baobab)

Arthur Brew Drive

Simuliapongo

Chabebi

Manjalide Drive

Rainbow Chalets
Police
T1
Zambezi
Flood Monument
Rainbow Lodge
Musi-O-Tunya International
Field Museum
Eastern Cataract
Knife Edges
Rainbow Falls
Boiling Pot
Katonta Pools
Danger Point
Namakabwa
Bungee Jumping
The Falls Bridge
Second Gorge
Third Gorge
Fifth Gorge
Zambezi

Princess Helena-Victoria Island
Nanvuvu Island
Princess Victoria Island
Main Falls
Rain Forest
White Water Rafting
Fourth Gorge

Namatobwe Island
Princess Marie Louise Island
Princess Christian Island
Cataract Island
Devil's Cataract
Entrance
Makasa Sun & Casino
Victoria Falls Station
Victoria Falls

Victoria Falls National Park

Big Tree
David Livingstone Monument
Ilala Lodge
Mallett

Zambezi Drive

Riverside

Marambs

Princess Elizabeth Island

Kalai Island

Z a m b e z

A'Zambezi River Lodge

Victoria Falls Boat Club

Entrance Gate
Park Tourist Office

Elephant Hills

ZIMBABWE

VICTORIA FALLS

Courtney Selous Cres. Rainbow
Dale Dr.
Park Way
West Dr.
Sopers Cres.
LIVINGSTONE
Spencer Rd.
Pioneer Road
Sprayview
A8

Victoria Falls Safari Lodge

Sprayview Airport

Zambezi National Park

BULAWAYO ROAD

To Bulawayo

Copyright ©Map Studio

Copyright ©Map Studio

Symbol	Legend			
Capital or City	Secondary Town	Major Airport	Place of Interest	Toll Route
Chief Administrative Town	Other Town	Airfield	Historical Site	Toll Plaza
Major Town	Settlement	Accommodation	Border Control	Major Spot Height

Game & Nature Reserves
Marsh
Waterfall

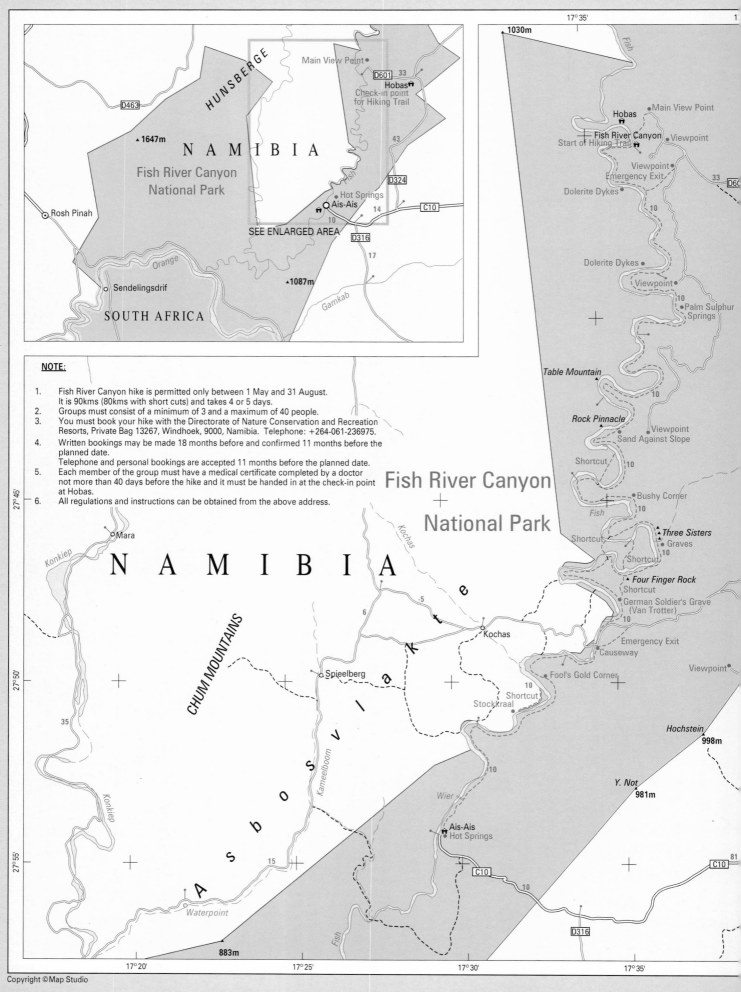

Scale 1 : 185 000

0 1 2 3 4 5 10k

NOTE:

1. Fish River Canyon hike is permitted only between 1 May and 31 August.
    It is 90kms (80kms with short cuts) and takes 4 or 5 days.
2. Groups must consist of a minimum of 3 and a maximum of 40 people.
3. You must book your hike with the Directorate of Nature Conservation and Recreation
    Resorts, Private Bag 13267, Windhoek, 9000, Namibia. Telephone: +264-061-236975.
4. Written bookings may be made 18 months before and confirmed 11 months before the
    planned date.
    Telephone and personal bookings are accepted 11 months before the planned date.
5. Each member of the group must have a medical certificate completed by a doctor
    not more than 40 days before the hike and it must be handed in at the check-in point
    at Hobas.
6. All regulations and instructions can be obtained from the above address.

under / untarred — Freeway & National Road / Principal Trunk Road
R523 — under / untarred — Main Road / Secondary Road
15 / 22 — Distances in Kilometres / Mountain Passes
Railway / International & Provincial Bound

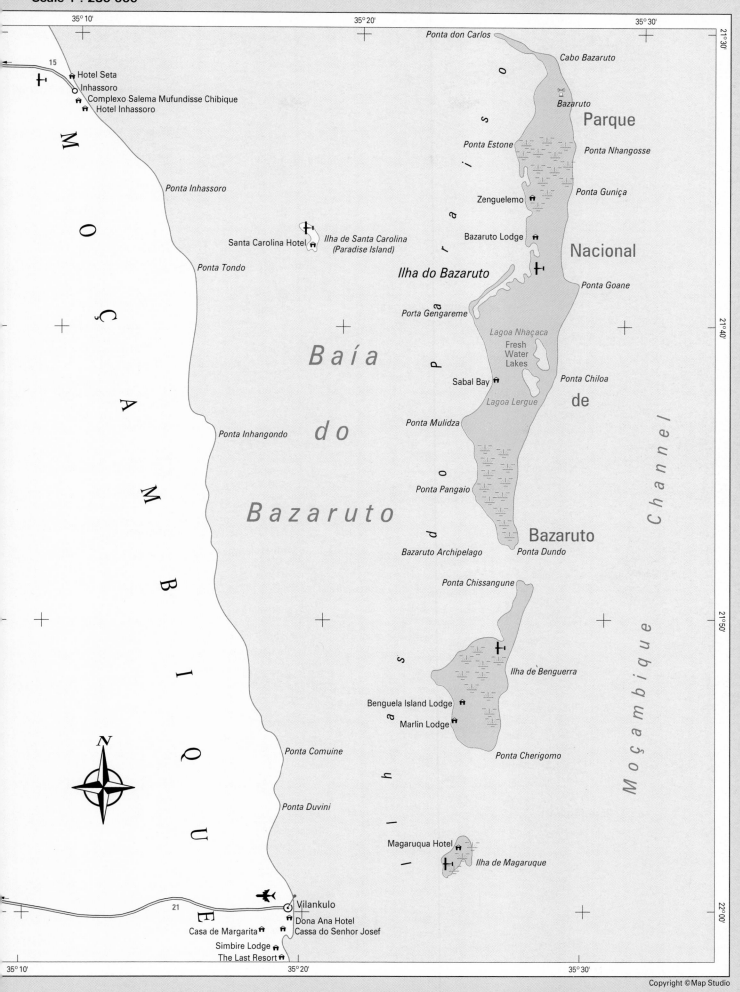

Scale 1 : 230 000

0 1 2 4 6 8 10km

35° 10' 35° 20' 35° 30'

Ponta don Carlos
Cabo Bazaruto
Bazaruto
Parque
Ponta Estone
Ponta Nhangosse
Ponta Guniça
Zenguelemo
Bazaruto Lodge
Nacional
Ilha do Bazaruto
Ponta Goane
Porta Gengareme
Lagoa Nhaçaca
Fresh Water Lakes
Sabal Bay
Ponta Chiloa
Lagoa Lergue
de
Ponta Mulidza
Ponta Pangaio
Bazaruto
Bazaruto Archipelago
Ponta Dundo

15
Hotel Seta
Inhassoro
Complexo Salema Mufundisse Chibique
Hotel Inhassoro

Ponta Inhassoro

Santa Carolina Hotel
Ilha de Santa Carolina
(Paradise Island)
Ponta Tondo

Baía
do
Bazaruto

Ponta Inhangondo

M
O
Ç
A
M
B
I
Q
U
E

Moçambique Channel

Ponta Chissangune

Ilha de Benguerra
Benguela Island Lodge
Marlin Lodge
Ponta Cherigomo

Ponta Comuine

Ponta Duvini

N

Magaruqua Hotel
Ilha de Magaruque

21

Vilankulo
Dona Ana Hotel
Casa de Margarita
Cassa do Senhor Josef
Simbire Lodge
The Last Resort

21° 30'
21° 40'
21° 50'
22° 00'

35° 10' 35° 20' 35° 30'

Copyright ©Map Studio

Capital or City
Chief Administrative Town
Major Town
Secondary Town
Other Town
Settlement
Major Airport
Airfield
Accommodation
Place of Interest
Historical Site
Border Control
Toll Route
Toll Plaza
Major Spot Height
Game & Nature Reserves
Marsh
Waterfall

Scale 1 : 5 970 000

0   50   100   150   200

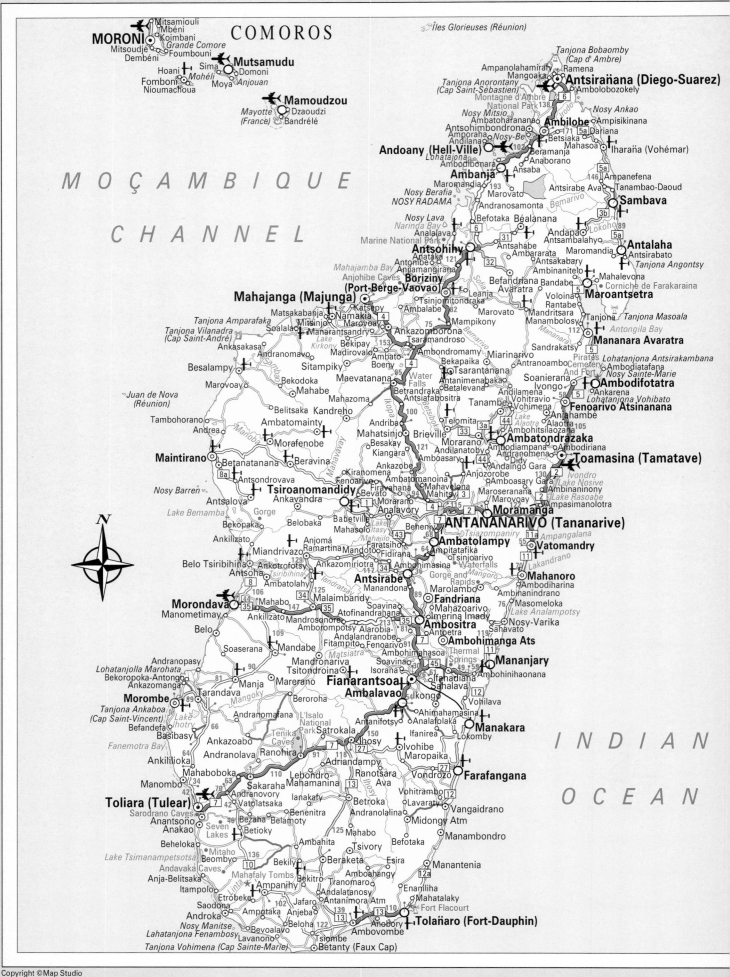

COMOROS

Îles Glorieuses (Réunion)

MORONI
Mitsamiouli
Mbéni
Koimbani
Mitsoudjé *Grande Comore*
Foumbouni
Dembéni

Mutsamudu
Sima
Hoani *Mohéli* Domoni
Fomboni Moya *Anjouan*
Nioumachoua

Mamoudzou
Mayotte (France) Dzaoudzi
Bandrélé

Tanjona Bobaomby (Cap d' Ambre)
Ramena
Ampanolahamiratry Mangoaka
Antsirañana (Diego-Suarez)
Tanjona Anorontany (Cap Saint-Sébastien) Ambolobozokely
Montagne d'Ambre National Park 138
Nosy Mitsio
Nosy Ankao
Antsohimbondrona 171 5a Dariana
Amporaha *Nosy-Be* Betsiaka Mahasoa
Andilana Beramanja Iharaña (Vohémar)
Andoany (Hell-Ville) Anaborano 5a
Lohatajona Ansaba
Ambodibonara 146 Ampanefena
Ambanja Antsirabe Ava Tanambao-Daoud
Maromandia 193
Marovato Sambava
Nosy Berafia Andranosamonta 3b
NOSY RADAMA Befotaka Béalanana Andapa 89 5a
Nosy Lava Antsahabe Antsambalahy Antalaha
Narinda Bay Analalava 31 Ambararata Antsakabary Maromandia Antsirabato
Marine National Park 6 Ambinanitelo *Tanjona Angontsy*
Antsohihy Befandriana Bandabe Mahalevona
Anataka 121 Avaratra Volana • *Corniche de Farakaraina*
Boriziny 32 Rantabe 5 Maroantsetra
(Port-Berge-Vaovao) Antombe Tsinjomitondraka Mandritsara *Tanjona* *Tanjona Masoala*
Mahajamba Bay Andilamangirana Leanja 82 Manambolosy 112 *Antongila Bay*
Anjohibe Caves Sofia Marovato
Mahajanga (Majunga) Mampikony Sandrakatsy Mananara Avaratra
Katsepy Ankazomborona *Pirates* *Lohatanjona Antsirakambana*
Matsakabanja Tsaramandroso Antranoambo Cemetery Ambodiatafana
Namakia 4 Ambondromamy And Fort *Nosy Sainte-Marie*
Mitsinjo Marovoay Bekapaika Ivongo Soanierana Ambodifotatra
Soalala Manarantsandry 153 Miarinarivo Andilamena Vohitravio 58
Bekipay Betrandraka Antanimenabaka Vohimena Fenoarivo Atsinanana
Andranomavo Madirovalo Ambato Antsiafabositra Ankarena 5 Anjahambe
Besalampy Sitampiky Boeny 85 Betalevana *Lake* Didy Fenoarivo
Bekodoka Maevatanana Tanamby *Alaotra* 105
Lake Mahabe Telomita Alaotra
Kirkony Ambohitsilaozana
Marovoay Belitsaka Kandreho Andriba Brieville 33 3a Ambatondrazaka
Ambatomainty Mahatsinjo 100 Morarano 44 Andranomena Ambodiriana
Tamborano Besakay 121 Ambodiampana Ambodiharina Toamasina (Tamatave)
Andrea Morafenobe Kiangara Andilanatoby 44 Andaingo Gara 130 Ivondro
Kiranomena Ankazobe Amboasary 2 Ambinaninony Gara *Lake Nosive*
Maintirano Betanatanana Ambatomanoina Ambato Marosny Maroseranana *Lake Rasoabe*
8a Antsondrovava Fenoarivo Firavahana Mahavelona Marovoay 2 Ampasimanolotra
Antsalova Ankavandra Bevato Mahitsy 3 Moramanga
Nosy Barren Tsiroanomandidy 1 Morarano 4 115
Bekopaka Belobaka Analavory 2 Vatomandry
Lake Bemamba Gorge *Lake* ANTANANARIVO (Tananarive) 55 11a *Ampangalana*
Ankilizato Babetville *Tsiazompaniry* Ambatolampy Manamoro
Miandrivazo Anjomá Behenjy 68 Ampitatafika 70 11
Belo Tsiribihina Ramartina 129 Faratsiho 64 *Waterfalls* *Lakandrano*
Antsoha Ankotrofotsy Mandoto Tsinjoarivo Mahanoro
8 Ambatolahy 117 Ankazomiriotra 34 Ambohimasina Gorge and Mangoro Ambodiharina
106 Malaimbandy 36 *Rapids* Ambinanindrano
Morondava 35 Mahabo Atofinandrahana 35 Antsirabe Manandona 89 Marolambo 76 *Lake Analampotsy*
Manometimay 147 Soavina Olmerina Imady Masomeloka
Ankilizato Mandrosonoro 213 Fandriana Nosy-Varika
Belo 109 Amborompotsy Alarobia Mahazoarivo 35
Soaserana Fitampito Fenoarivo 91 Ambositra 81 Ambohimanga Ats
Mandabe Andalandranobe Antoetra 7 119
Andranopasy Mandronariva Soavina 7 *Thermal*
Lohatanjolla Marohata Tsitondroina Isorana Ambohimahasoa *Springs* 11
Bekoropoka-Antongo Manja Marerano Ambohinihaonana Mananjary
Ankazomanga 81 45 49 55
Morombe Tarandava Fianarantsoa Ifanadiana
Tanjona Ankaboa Beroroha Ambalavao Sahalava 12
(Cap Saint-Vincent) Andranomafana Ikongo Vohilava
Befandefa *L'Isalo* 54
Basibasy *National* Satrokala Ahimahamasina Manakara
Fanemotra Bay *Park* 150 Antanifotsy Analafolaka
Tenika Ranohira 7 Ihosy Ifanirea Lokomby
Caves 118 Adriandampy 27 Ivohibe
Ankililioka Andranolava 91 Maropaika 27
Mahaboboka 63 Lebondro 13 Vondrozo Farafangana
Manombo Sakaraha 110 Mahamanina Ranotsara
42 Andranovory Ianakafy Ava Vohitrambo 12
Toliara (Tulear) 7 42 Vatolatsaka Betroka Lavaraty Vangaidrano
Sarodrano Caves Bezaha Andranolalina
Anantsono Benenitra Mahabo Midongy Atm Manambondro
Anakao 46 Betioky 125 Befotaka
Beheloka Mitaho Bekily Tsivory Manantenia
Lake Tsimanampetsots Beomby Andalatanosy 12a
Andavaka Caves 136 Bekitro Tranomaro Enanliha
Anja-Belitsaka 10 Berakéta Esira Mahatalaky
Itampolo Mahafaly Tombs Amboahangy *Fort Flacourt*
Saodona Ampanihy Antanimora Atm 10
Androka 102 Jafaro Anjeba 13 13 110 Tolañaro (Fort-Dauphin)
Nosy Manitse 139 Anobory
Lahatanjona Fenamboy Bevoalavo Beloha 122 Ambovombe
Tanjona Vohimena (Cap Sainte-Marie) Lavanono Tsiombe Betanty (Faux Cap)

MOÇAMBIQUE

CHANNEL

Juan de Nova (Réunion)

N

INDIAN

OCEAN

Copyright ©Map Studio

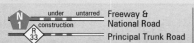

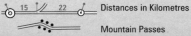

	under	untarred			Freeway & National Road
N1	construction				
R33					Principal Trunk Road

R523	under	untarred	Main Road
	construction		
			Secondary Road

15 | 22 | Distances in Kilometres
Mountain Passes

Railway
International & Provincial Boun

2 4 6 8 10km
cale 1 : 356 000

Copyright ©Map Studio

▪ Capital or City	⊙ Secondary Town	✈ Major Airport	• Place of Interest	Ⓣ Toll Route	Game & Nature Reserves
Chief Administrative Town	⊙ Other Town	Ⓗ Airfield	★ Historical Site	Ⓣ Toll Plaza	Marsh
▪ Major Town	○ Settlement	Ⓗ Accommodation	✦ Border Control	▲ Major Spot Height	Waterfall

Scale 1 : 284 000

0   2   4   6   8   10

INDIAN OCEAN

Copyright ©Map Studio

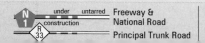

Freeway &
National Road

Principal Trunk Road

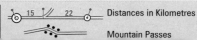

Main Road

Secondary Road

15 ⊙ 22   Distances in Kilometres

Mountain Passes

Railway

International &
Provincial Boundary

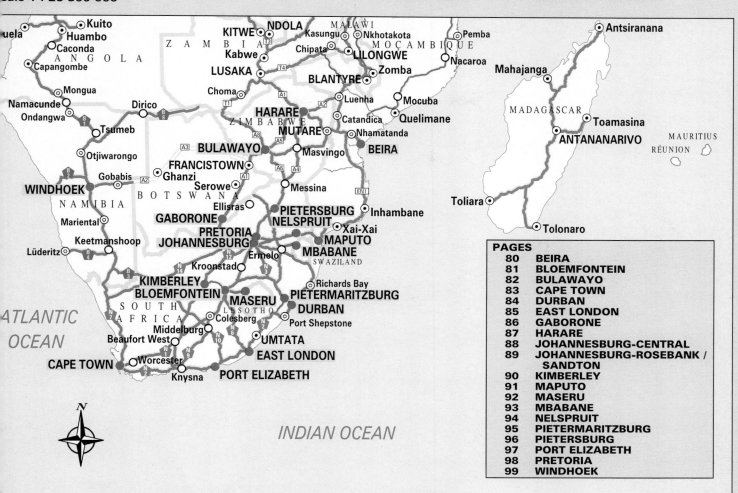

200	400	600km

Scale 1 : 25 500 000

LEGEND TO STREET MAPS

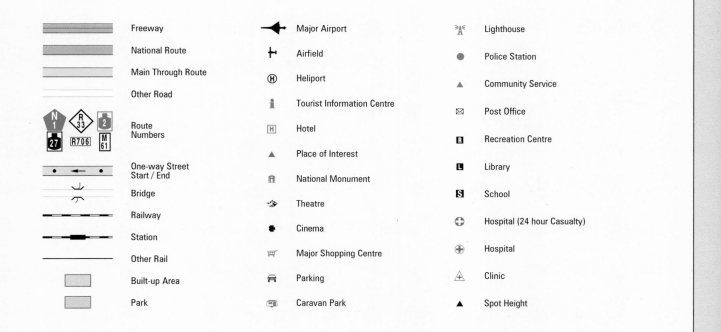

Freeway

National Route

Main Through Route

Other Road

Route Numbers

One-way Street Start / End

Bridge

Railway

Station

Other Rail

Built-up Area

Park

Major Airport

Airfield

Heliport

Tourist Information Centre

Hotel

Place of Interest

National Monument

Theatre

Cinema

Major Shopping Centre

Parking

Caravan Park

Lighthouse

Police Station

Community Service

Post Office

Recreation Centre

Library

School

Hospital (24 hour Casualty)

Hospital

Clinic

Spot Height

Copyright ©Map Studio

0 200 400 600
Scale 1 : 20 000

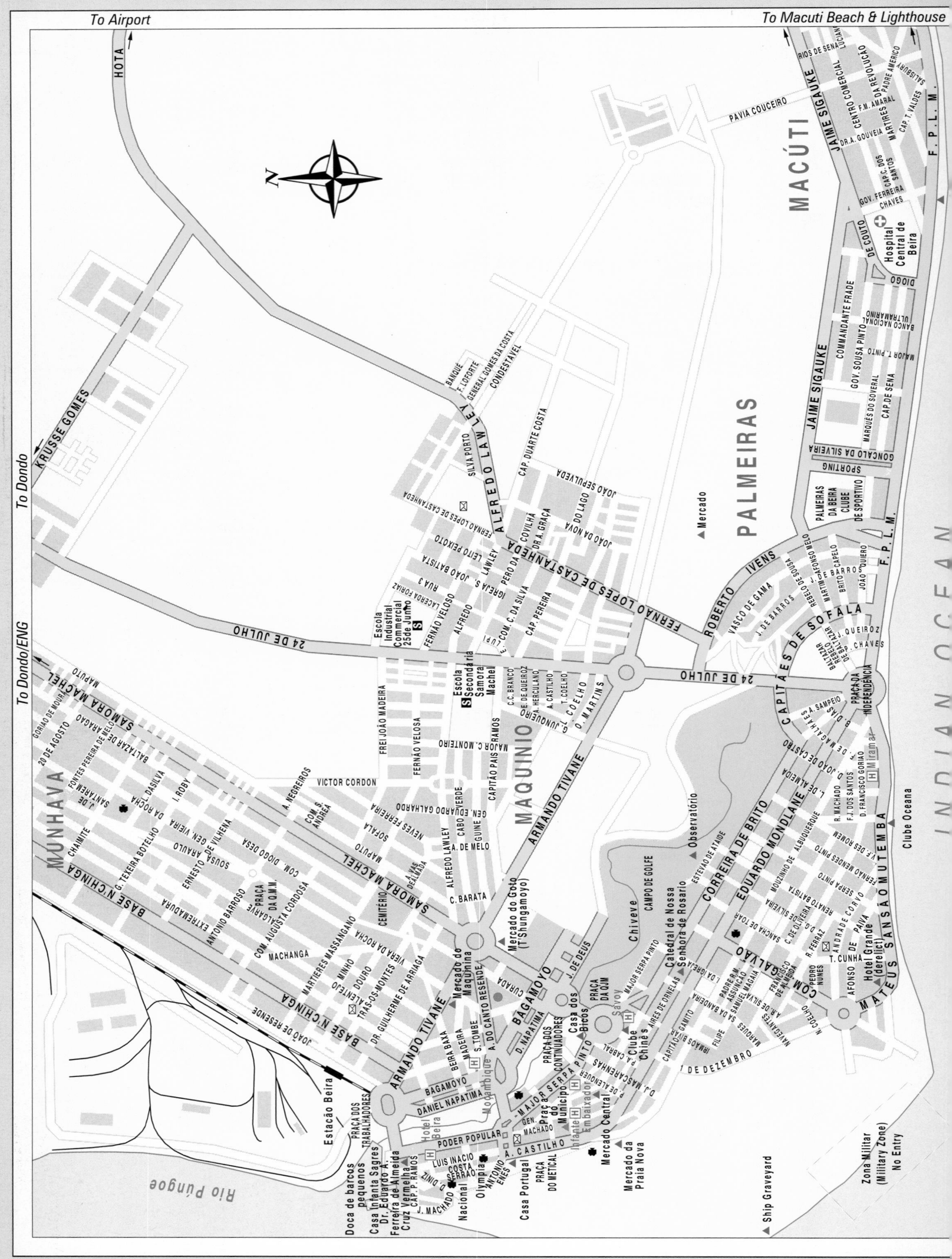

To Airport
To Macuti Beach & Lighthouse
To Dondo
To Dondo/ENG
HOTA
KRUSSE GOMES
MACÚTI
PALMEIRAS
MAQUINIO
MUNHAVA
MACHANGA
INDIAN OCEAN
Rio Púngoe
PAVIA COUCEIRO
JAIME SIGAUKE
F.P.L.M.
CENTRO COMERCIAL
DA REVOLUÇÃO
Hospital Central de Beira
DE COUTO
DIOGO
COMMANDANTE FRADE
BANCO NACIONAL ULTRAMARINO
GOV. SOUSA PINTO
MAJOR T. PINTO
MARQUÊS DO SOVERAL
CAP. DE SENA
GONÇALO DA SILVEIRA
SPORTING
PALMEIRAS DA BEIRA CLUBE DE SPORTIVO
Mercado
ROBERTO IVENS
VASCO DA GAMA
CAPITÃES DE SOFALA
PRAÇA DA INDEPENDÊNCIA
24 DE JULHO
FERNÃO LOPES DE CASTANHEDA
ALFREDO LAWLEY
CAP. DUARTE COSTA
JOÃO SEPULVEDA
DO LAGO
JOÃO DA NOVA
LEITO PEIXOTO
JOÃO BATISTA
RUA 3
LACERDA FORIAZ
FERNÃO VELOSO
Escola Industrial Commercial 25de Junho
Escola Secundária Samora Machel
SILVA PORTO
CONDESTAVEL
GENERAL GOMES DA COSTA
F. LOFORTE
BANQUE
FREI JOÃO MADEIRA
FERNÃO VELOSA
MAJOR C. MONTEIRO
CAPITÃO PAIS RAMOS
VICTOR CORDON
ARMANDO TIVANE
SAMORA MACHEL
BASE N'CHINGA
MAPUTO
NEVES FERREIRA
SOFALA
CABO VERDE
GUINÉ
A. DE MELO
ALFREDO LAWLEY
C. BARATA
CEMITÉRIO
Mercado do Goto (T'Shungamoyo)
Mercado do Maquinina
Observatório
CAMPO DE GOLFE
Chiveve
Catedral de Nossa Senhora de Rosario
CORREIRA DE BRITO
EDUARDO MONDLANE
SANSÃO MUTEMBA
MATEUS
Clube Oceana
Hotel Grande (derelict)
Zona Militar (Military Zone) No Entry
Ship Graveyard
Mercado da Praia Nova
Mercado Central
BAGAMOYO
DANIEL NAPATIMA
PODER POPULAR
A. CASTILHO
MAJOR SERPA PINTO
Praça do Municipio
Casa Portugal
PRAÇA DO METICAL
Estacão Beira
PRAÇA DOS TRABALHADORES
Doca de barcos pequenos
Casa Infanta Sagres
Dr. Eduardo A. Ferreira de Almeida
Cruz Vermelha
Nacional
Olympia
Hotel Beira
Moçambique
Savoy
Clube Chinês
Casa dos Bicos
PRAÇA DA OJM
1 DE DEZEMBRO
COM. GALVÃO
Miramar

Copyright ©Map Studio

Freeway
National Route
Main Through Route
Other Road
Route Numbers
One-way Street
Start / End
Bridge
Railway
Station
Other Rail
Built-up Area
Park

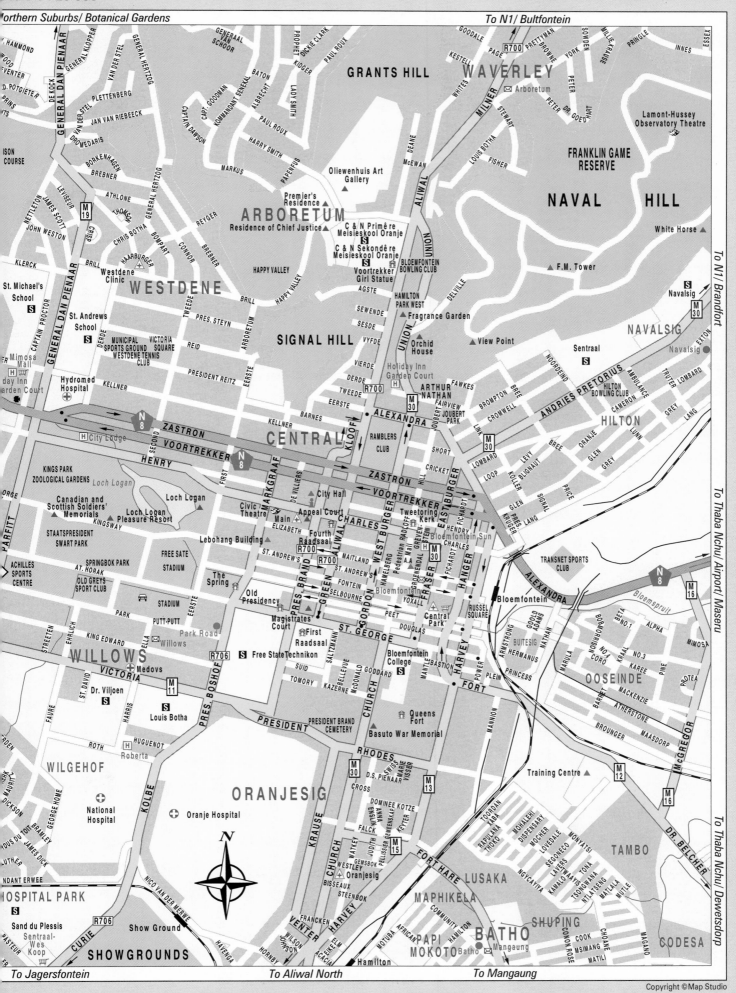

Scale 1 : 20 000

To N1/ Bultfontein

To N1 /Brandfort

To Thaba Nchu/ Airport/ Maseru

To Thaba Nchu /Dewetsdorp

To Jagersfontein

To Aliwal North

To Mangaung

Copyright ©Map Studio

Major Airport	Tourist Information Centre	National Monument	Police Station	Recreation Centre	Hospital (24 hour Casualty)	Parking
Airfield	Hotel	Theatre	Community Service	Library	Hospital	Caravan Park
Heliport	Place of Interest	Cinema	Post Office	School	Clinic	Major Shopping Centre

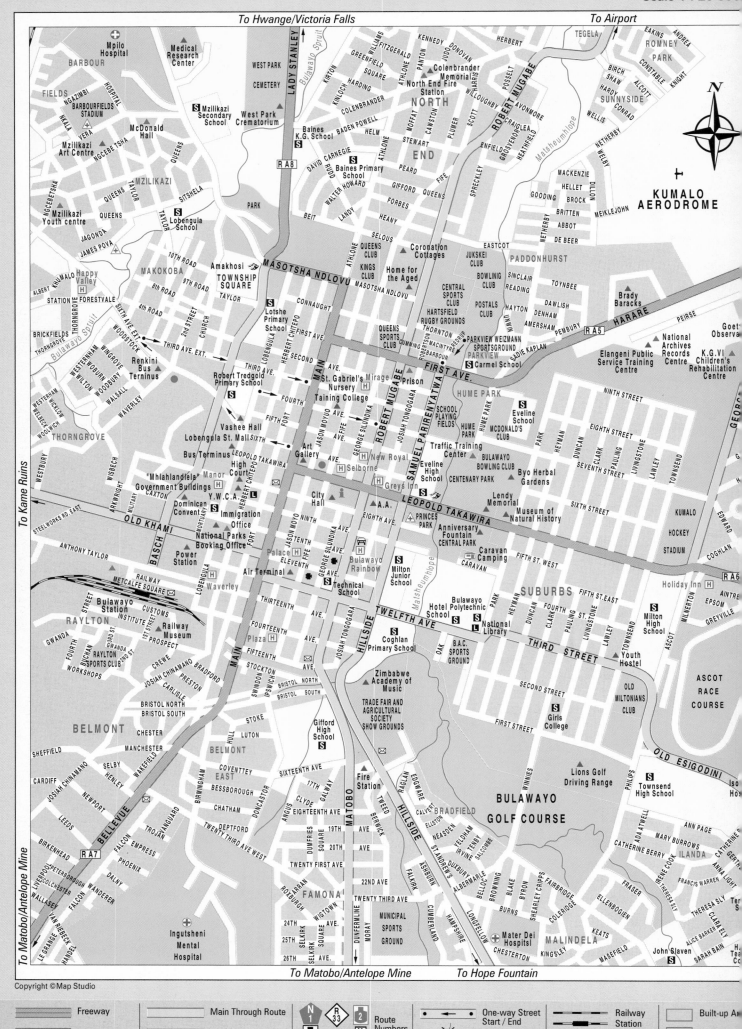

Scale 1 : 20 000

Copyright ©Map Studio

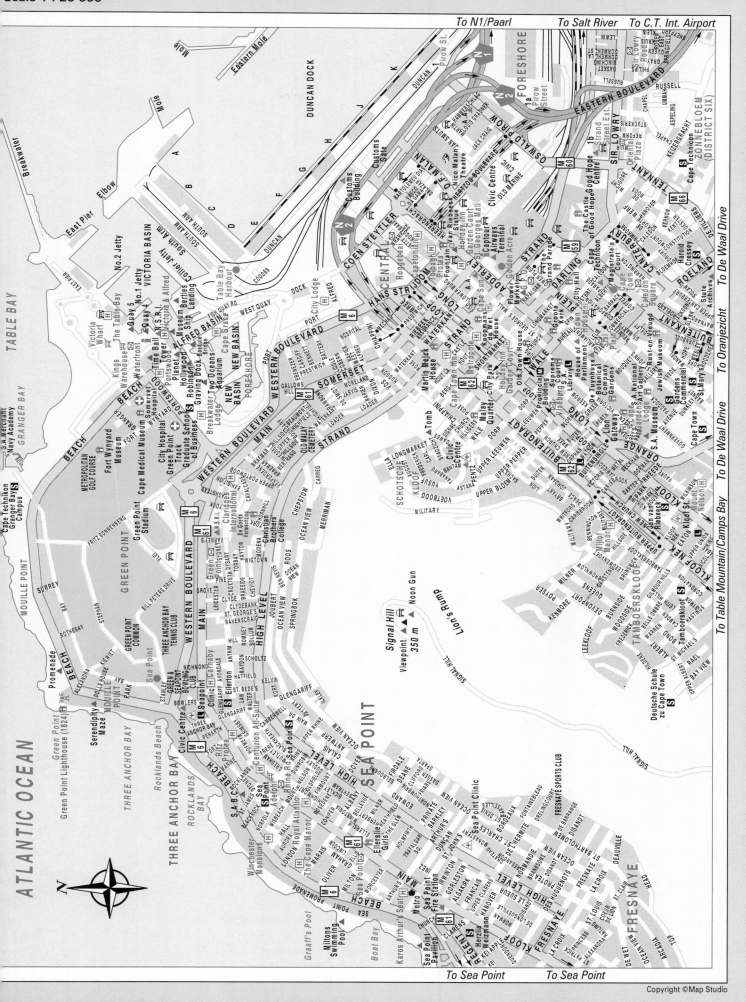

Scale 1 : 20 000

Major Airport	i Tourist Information Centre	⌂ National Monument	● Police Station	R Recreation Centre	✚ Hospital (24 hour Casualty)	🚗 Parking
Airfield	H Hotel	✈ Theatre	▲ Community Service	L Library	✚ Hospital	Caravan Park
Heliport	▲ Place of Interest	🎬 Cinema	✉ Post Office	S School	▲ Clinic	Major Shopping Centre

Copyright ©Map Studio

Scale 1 : 20 000

0   200   400   6

INDIAN OCEAN

BAY OF NATAL

Copyright © Map Studio

▬▬▬ Freeway	▬▬▬ Main Through Route	Route Numbers	◄●—► One-way Street Start / End	▬▬▬ Railway	Built-up Area
▬▬▬ National Route	▬▬▬ Other Road		⌣ Bridge	▬▬▬ Other Rail	Park

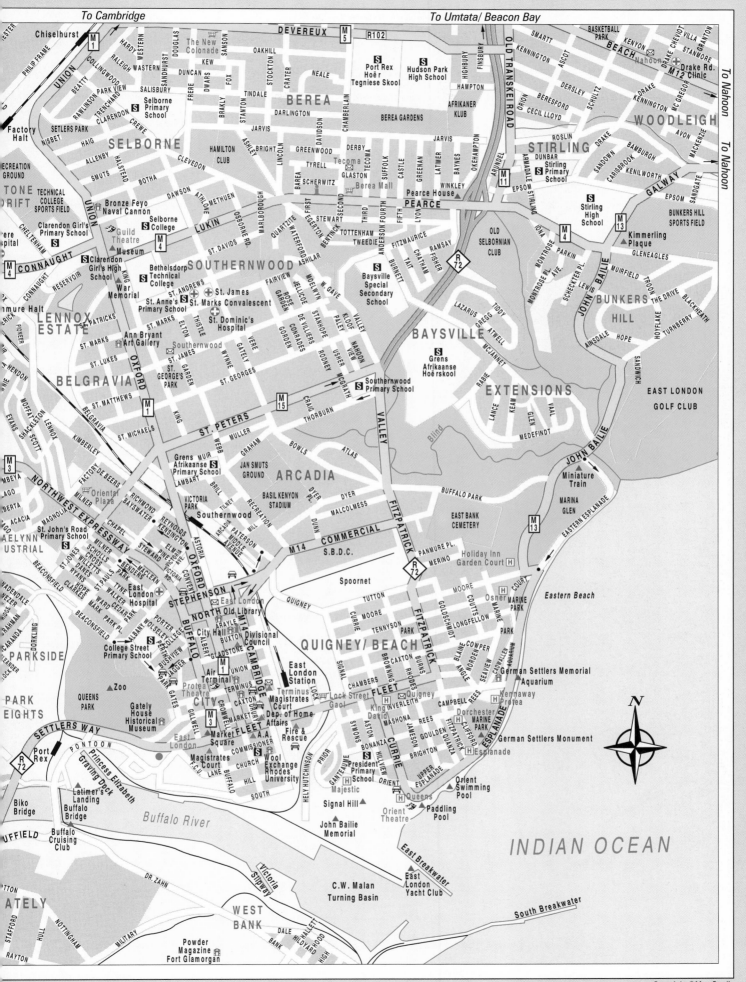

Scale 1 : 20 000

200 400 600m

To Cambridge | To Umtata/ Beacon Bay | To Nahoon | To Nahoon

INDIAN OCEAN

Buffalo River

Copyright ©Map Studio

▲ Major Airport | ℹ Tourist Information Centre | 🏛 National Monument | ● Police Station | R Recreation Centre | ✚ Hospital (24 hour Casualty) | 🅿 Parking
✈ Airfield | H Hotel | 🎭 Theatre | ▲ Community Service | L Library | ✚ Hospital | 🚐 Caravan Park
Heliport | ▲ Place of Interest | 🎬 Cinema | ✉ Post Office | S School | △ Clinic | 🏪 Major Shopping Centre

Copyright ©Map Studio

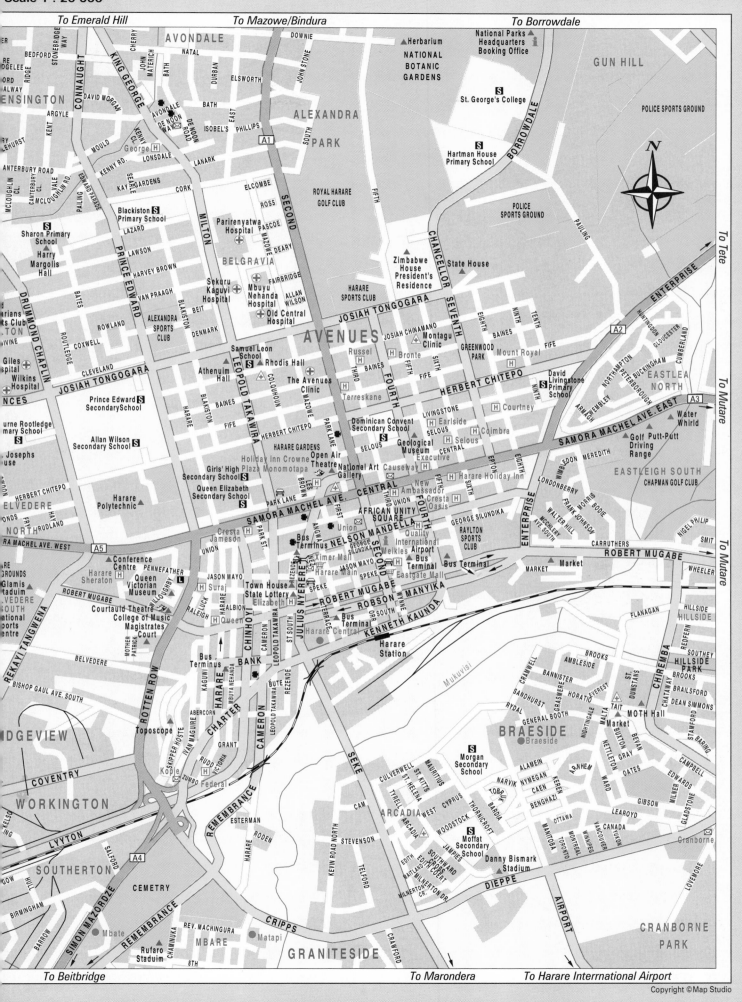

Scale 1 : 20 000
200 400 600m

To Emerald Hill   To Mazowe/Bindura   To Borrowdale

To Beitbridge   To Marondera   To Harare Interrnational Airport

Copyright ©Map Studio

✈ Major Airport   ℹ Tourist Information Centre   ⌂ National Monument   ● Police Station   R Recreation Centre   ✚ Hospital (24 hour Casualty)   🅿 Parking
Airfield   H Hotel   ✍ Theatre   ▲ Community Service   ⊠ Post Office   ✚ Hospital   Caravan Park
Heliport   ▲ Place of Interest   ✪ Cinema   ✉ Community Service   S School   △ Clinic   Major Shopping Centre
   L Library

Scale 1 : 20 000

Copyright ©Map Studio

Scale 1 : 25 000
200 400 600 800m

Scale 1 : 20 000

Copyright ©Map Studio

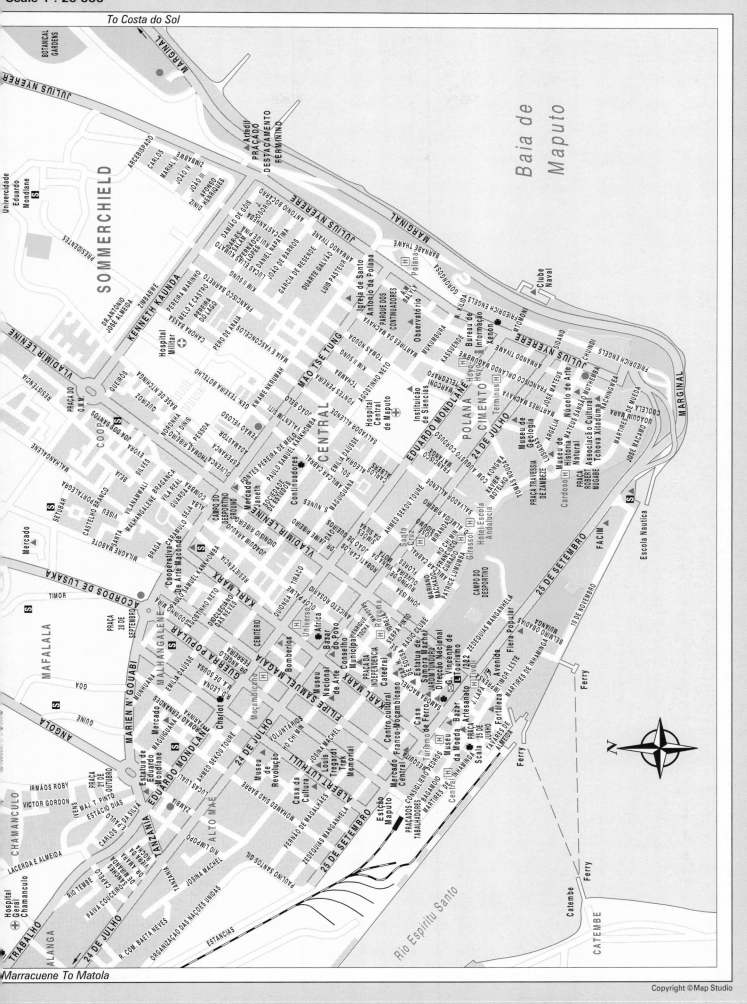

Scale 1 : 20 000
200 400 600m

To Costa do Sol

Baia de Maputo

Rio Espiritu Santo

Marracuene To Matola

Copyright ©Map Studio

← Major Airport	🛈 Tourist Information Centre	🏛 National Monument	● Police Station	Ⓡ Recreation Centre	✚ Hospital (24 hour Casualty)	🅿 Parking
Airfield	Ⓗ Hotel	✈ Theatre	▲ Community Service	Ⓛ Library	⊕ Hospital	Caravan Park
Heliport	▲ Place of Interest	✹ Cinema	✉ Post Office	Ⓢ School	△ Clinic	Major Shopping Centre

Scale 1 : 20 000

0   200   400   60

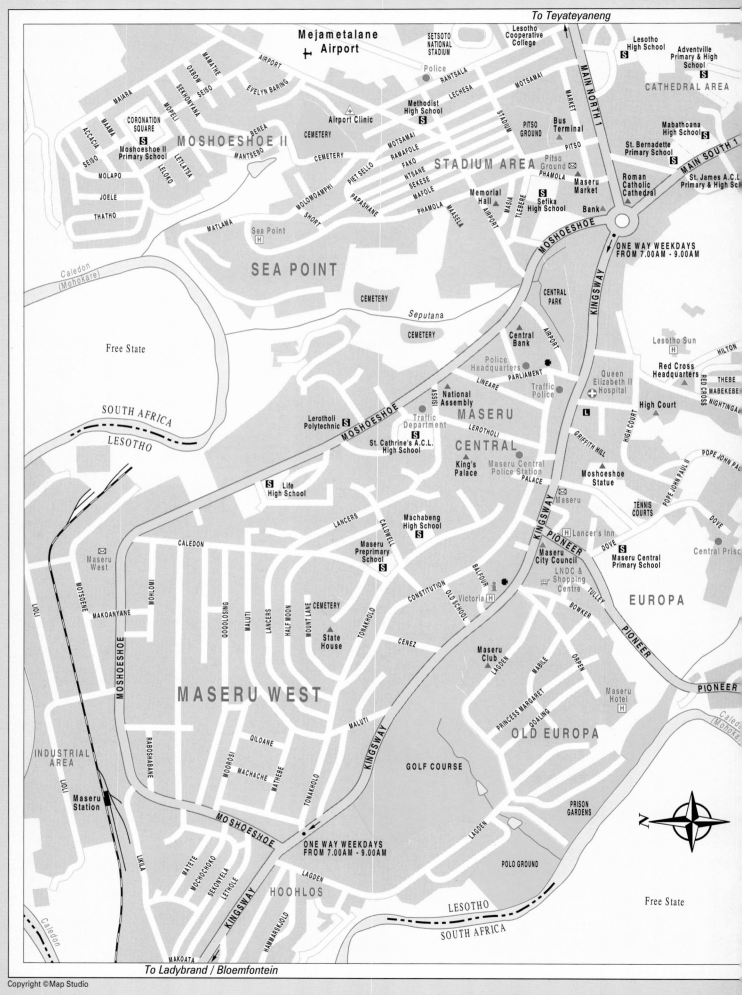

To Teyateyaneng

Mejametalane Airport

SETSOTO NATIONAL STADIUM

Lesotho Cooperative College

Police

Lesotho High School

Adventville Primary & High School

CATHEDRAL AREA

Rantsala

Methodist High School

MOSHOESHOE II

CORONATION SQUARE

Moshoeshoe II Primary School

Airport Clinic

CEMETERY

CEMETERY

Pitso Ground

Bus Terminal

Mabathoana High School

St. Bernadette Primary School

Roman Catholic Cathedral

St. James A.C.L Primary & High School

MAIN NORTH 1

MAIN SOUTH 1

MARKET

STADIUM AREA

STADIUM

Pitso Ground

PHAMOLA

Maseru Market

Memorial Hall

Sefika High School

Bank

SEA POINT

Sea Point

CALEDON (MOHOKARE)

FREE STATE

SOUTH AFRICA

LESOTHO

CEMETERY

Seputana

CEMETERY

CEMETERY

MOSHOESHOE

KINGSWAY

CENTRAL PARK

ONE WAY WEEKDAYS FROM 7.00AM - 9.00AM

Central Bank

Police Headquarters

PARLIAMENT

Traffic Police

AIRPORT

Lesotho Sun

HILTON

Red Cross Headquarters

Queen Elizabeth II Hospital

High Court

High Court

RED CROSS

THEBE

MABEKEBE

NIGHTINGALE

National Assembly

MASERU CENTRAL

Traffic Department

Lerotholi Polytechnic

St. Cathrine's A.C.L. High School

LINEARE

LEROTHOLI

King's Palace

Maseru Central Police Station

PALACE

Moshoeshoe Statue

GRIFFITH HILL

HIGH COURT

POPE JOHN PAUL II

TENNIS COURTS

POPE JOHN PAUL II

DOVE

Central Prison

Life High School

Machabeng High School

Maseru Preprimary School

LANCERS

CALDWELL

Maseru

Lancer's Inn

Maseru City Council

LNDC & Shopping Centre

Maseru Central Primary School

EUROPA

DOVE

CALEDON

MOSHOESHOE

MASERU WEST

LIOLI

MOTSOENE

MOHLOMI

MAKOANYANE

QOQOLOSING

MALUTI

LANCERS

HALF MOON

MOUNT LANE

CEMETERY

State House

TONAKHOLO

CONSTITUTION

OLD SCHOOL

CENEZ

BALFOUR

KINGSWAY

PIONEER

Victoria

Maseru Club

LAGDEN

MABILE

OPEN

PRINCESS MARGARET

Maseru Hotel

OLD EUROPA

PIONEER

PIONEER

BOWKER

TULLEY

Maseru West

INDUSTRIAL AREA

LIOLI

Maseru Station

RABOSHABANE

QILOANE

MOOROSI

MACHACHE

MATHEBE

MALUTI

TONAKHOLO

KINGSWAY

GOLF COURSE

OOALING

LAGDEN

PRISON GARDENS

MATETE

MOCHOCHOKO

SEKONYELA

LETHOLE

KINGSWAY

HAMMARSKJOLD

HOOHLOS

LAGDEN

ONE WAY WEEKDAYS FROM 7.00AM - 9.00AM

POLO GROUND

CALEDON (MOHOKARE)

Free State

MOSHOESHOE

MAKOATA

To Ladybrand / Bloemfontein

CALEDON

LESOTHO

SOUTH AFRICA

N

Copyright ©Map Studio

Freeway	Main Through Route	N1 R33 2 Route Numbers	One-way Street Start / End	Railway	Built-up Area
National Route	Other Road	27 R706 M61	Bridge	Station / Other Rail	Park

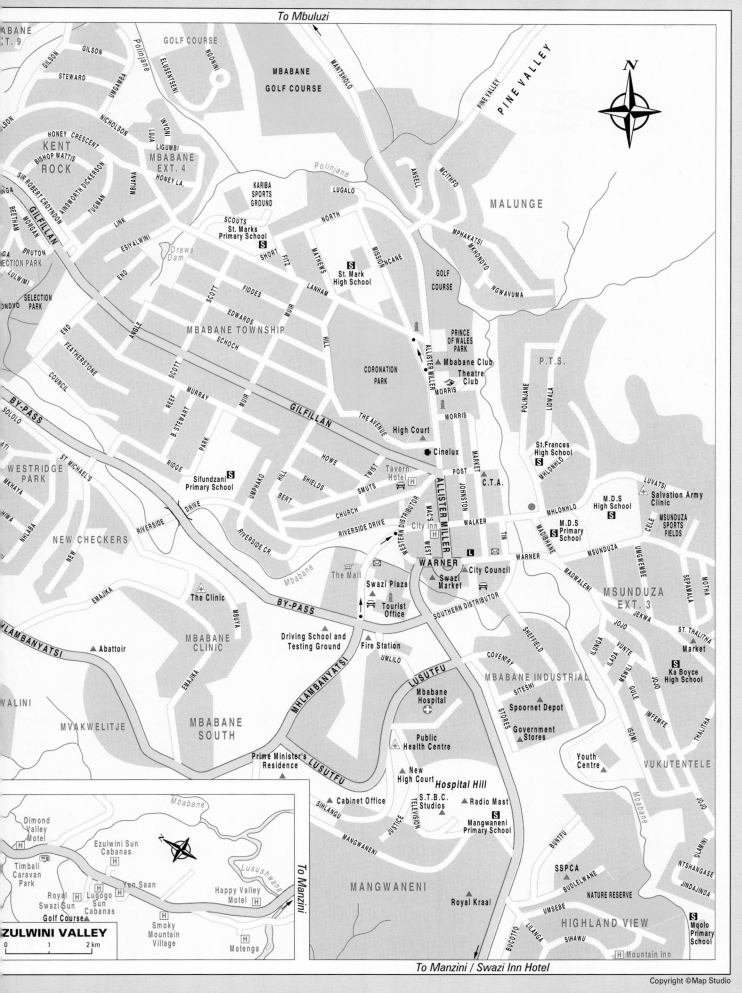

Scale 1 : 20 000
200 400 600m

To Mbuluzi

ZULWINI VALLEY
0   1   2 km

To Manzini / Swazi Inn Hotel

Copyright ©Map Studio

Major Airport	Tourist Information Centre	National Monument
Heliport	Hotel	Theatre
Place of Interest	Cinema	

Police Station	Recreation Centre	Hospital (24 hour Casualty)	Parking	
Community Service	Library	Hospital	Caravan Park	
Post Office	School	Clinic	Major Shopping Centre	

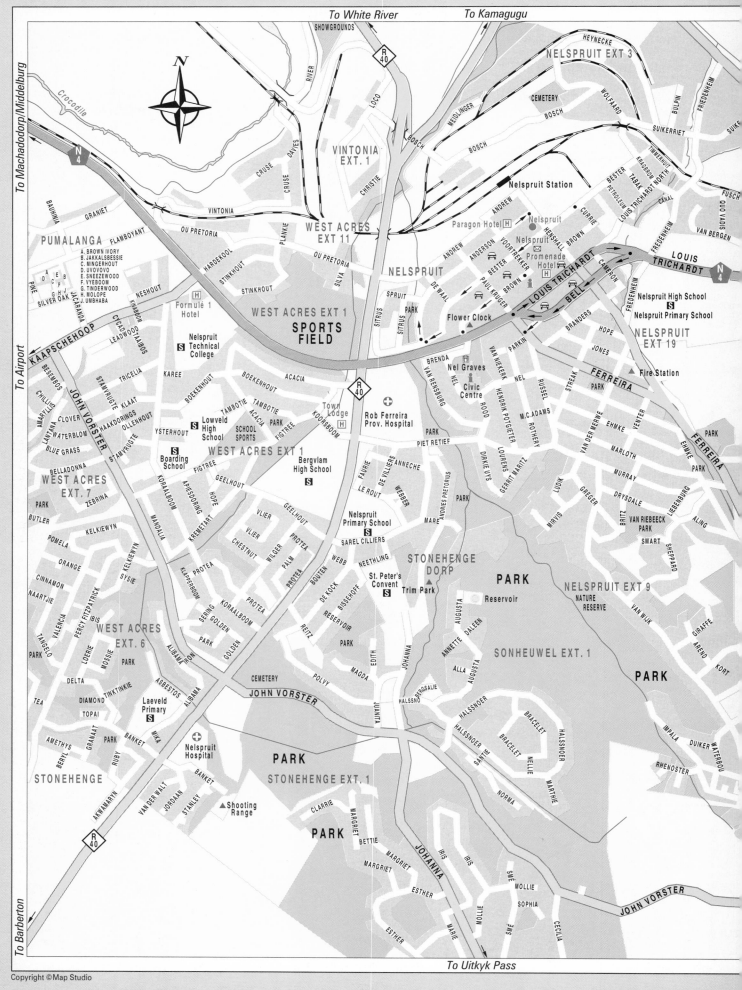

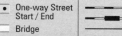

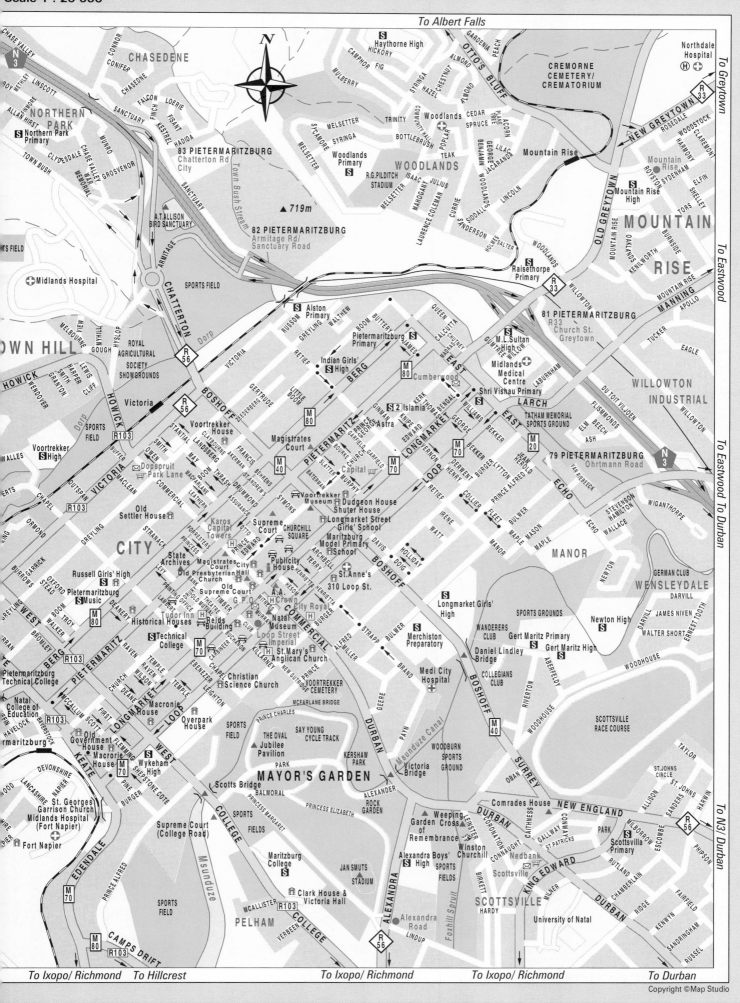

Scale 1 : 20 000

200 400 600m

To Albert Falls

To Greytown

To Eastwood

To Eastwood To Durban

To N3/ Durban

To Ixopo/ Richmond   To Hillcrest   To Ixopo/ Richmond   To Ixopo/ Richmond   To Durban

Copyright ©Map Studio

✈ Major Airport	ℹ Tourist Information Centre	🏛 National Monument	● Police Station	R Recreation Centre	✚ Hospital (24 hour Casualty)	🚗 Parking
Airfield	H Hotel	☆ Theatre	▲ Community Service	L Library	✚ Hospital	🚐 Caravan Park
Heliport	▲ Place of Interest	✖ Cinema	✉ Post Office	S School	△ Clinic	🛒 Major Shopping Centre

Copyright © Map Studio

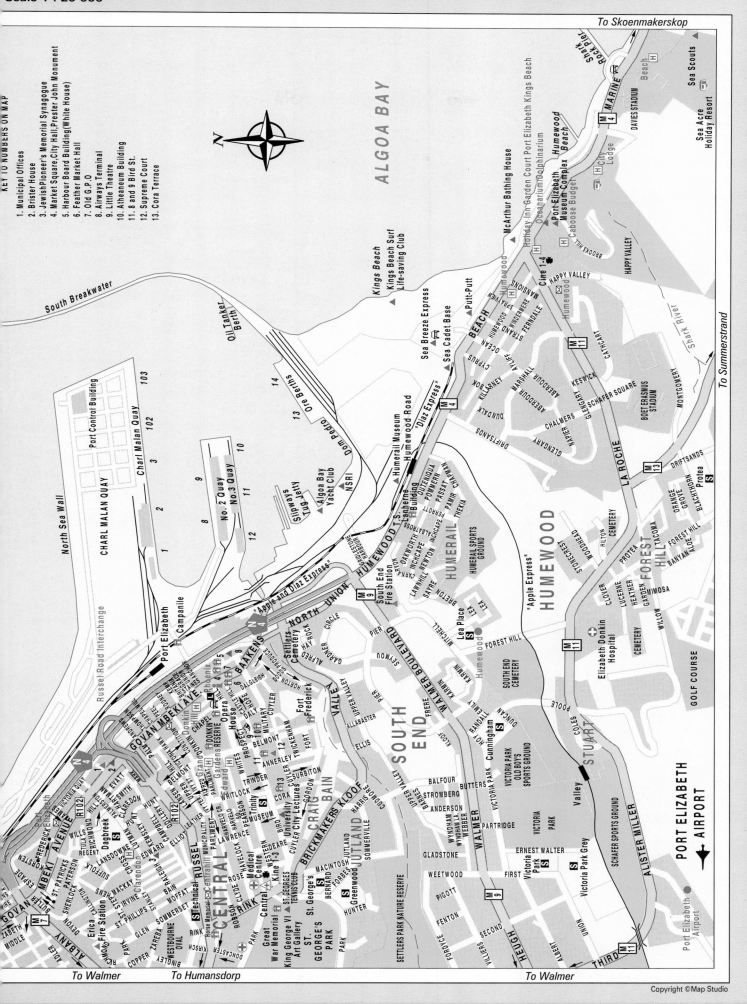

Scale 1 : 20 000

200 400 600m

To Skoenmakerskop

KEY TO NUMBERS ON MAP
1. Municipal Offices
2. Brister House
3. JewishPioneer's Memorial Synagogue
4. Market Square,City Hall,Prester John Monument
5. Harbour Board Building(White House)
6. Feather Market Hall
7. Old G.P.O
8. Airways Terminal
9. Little Theatre
10. Atheaneum Building
11. 8 and 9 Bird St.
12. Supreme Court
13. Cora Terrace

ALGOA BAY

To Summerstrand

To Walmer   To Humansdorp   To Walmer

Copyright ©Map Studio

⤴ Major Airport	ℹ Tourist Information Centre
✈ Airfield	H Hotel
Heliport	▲ Place of Interest

⌂ National Monument	● Police Station
Theatre	▲ Community Service
● Cinema	✉ Post Office

R Recreation Centre	✚ Hospital (24 hour Casualty)
L Library	✚ Hospital
S School	△ Clinic

P Parking	
Caravan Park	
Major Shopping Centre	

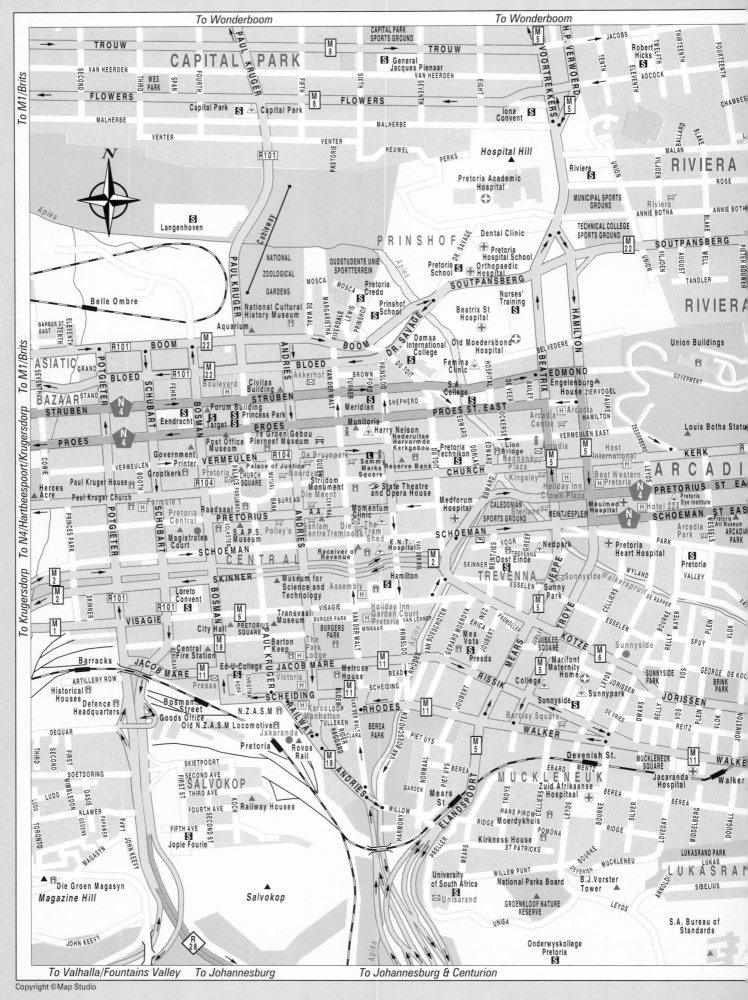

Copyright ©Map Studio

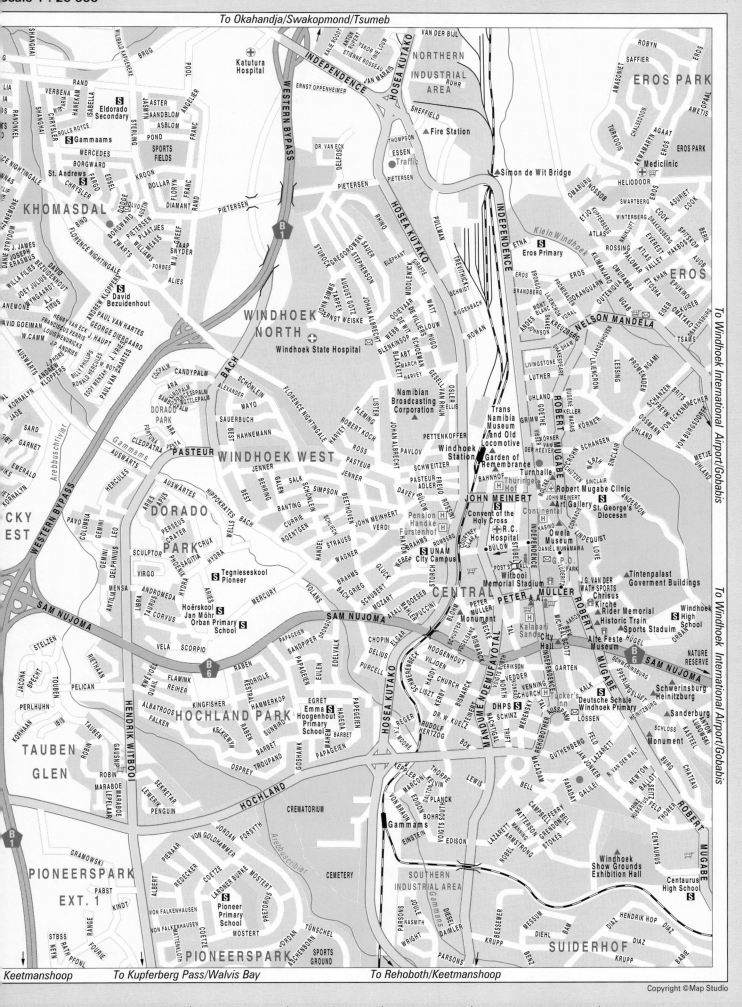

Scale 1 : 20 000

To Okahandja/Swakopmond/Tsumeb

Copyright ©Map Studio

✈ Major Airport	ℹ Tourist Information Centre	🏛 National Monument
Airfield	Ⓗ Hotel	🎭 Theatre
Heliport	▲ Place of Interest	🎬 Cinema
● Police Station	Ⓡ Recreation Centre	✚ Hospital (24 hour Casualty)
▲ Community Service	Ⓛ Library	⊕ Hospital
⊠ Post Office	Ⓢ School	△ Clinic
🚗 Parking		
🚐 Caravan Park		
🛒 Major Shopping Centre		

PAGE 101
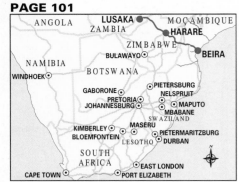
LUSAKA TO HARARE
HARARE TO BEIRA

PAGE 102
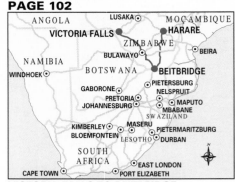
VICTORIA FALLS TO BEITBRIDGE
HARARE TO BEITBRIDGE

PAGE 103

JOHANNESBURG TO MAPUTO
MAPUTO TO DURBAN

PAGE 104
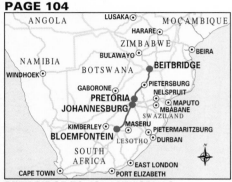
BEITBRIDGE TO JOHANNESBURG
PRETORIA TO BLOEMFONTEIN

PAGE 105

BLOEMFONTEIN TO CAPE TOWN
BLOEMFONTEIN TO PORT ELIZABETH

PAGE 106
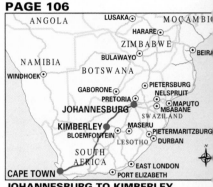
JOHANNESBURG TO KIMBERLEY
KIMBERLEY TO CAPE TOWN

PAGE 107
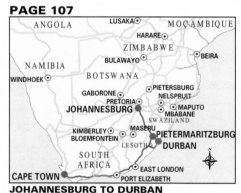
JOHANNESBURG TO DURBAN
PIETERMARITZBURG TO CAPE TOWN

PAGE 108
WINDHOEK TO CAPE TOWN
KEETMANSHOOP TO PORT ELIZABETH

LEGEND TO STRIP ROUTES

The strip route maps are a representation of features
to be found en route and are not drawn to scale
Kilometre distances are given in black figures,
depending on direction of travel.

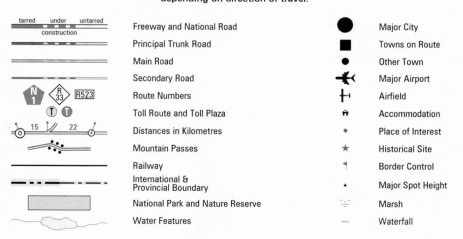

Freeway and National Road	Major City
Principal Trunk Road	Towns on Route
Main Road	Other Town
Secondary Road	Major Airport
Route Numbers	Airfield
Toll Route and Toll Plaza	Accommodation
Distances in Kilometres	Place of Interest
Mountain Passes	Historical Site
Railway	Border Control
International & Provincial Boundary	Major Spot Height
National Park and Nature Reserve	Marsh
Water Features	Waterfall

Copyright ©Map Studio

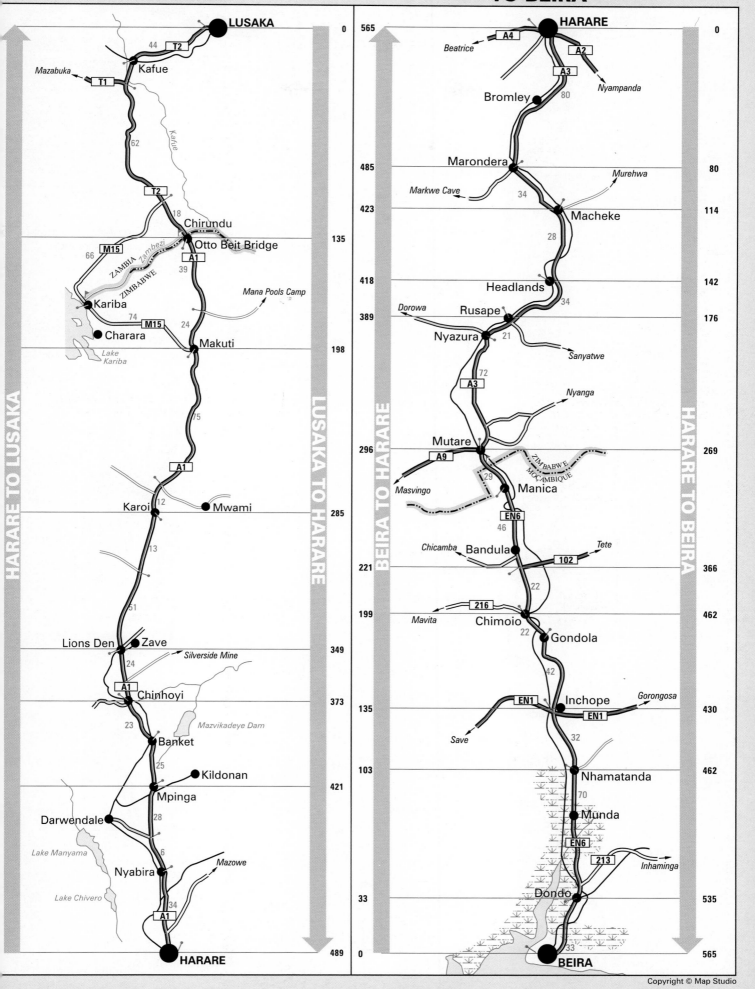

Copyright © Map Studio

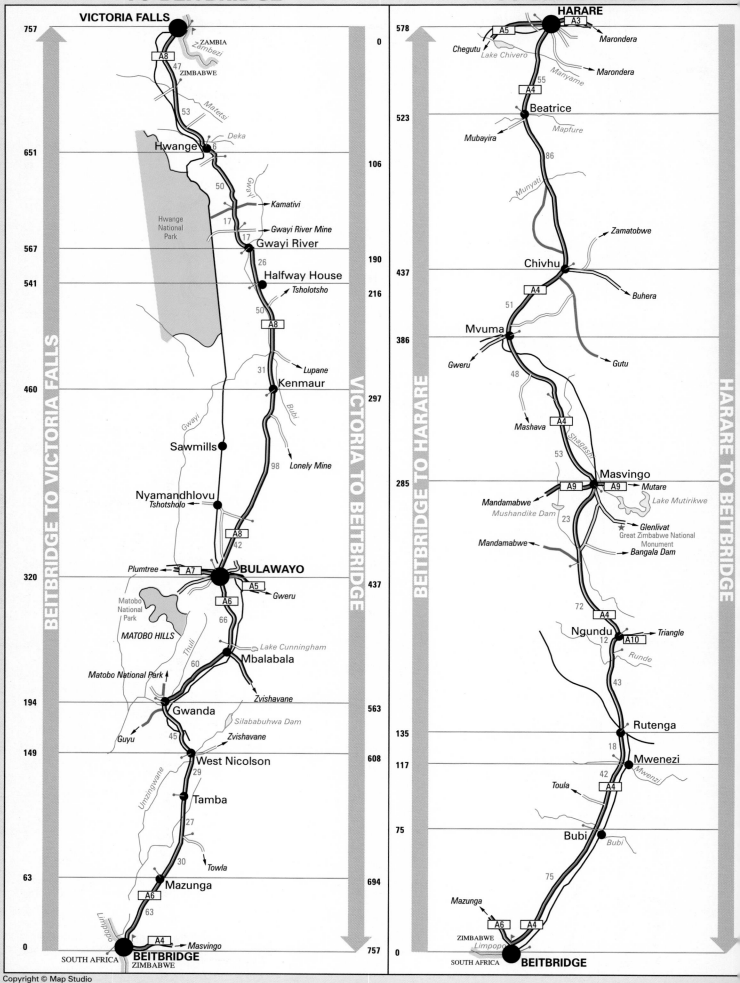

BEITBRIDGE TO VICTORIA FALLS

VICTORIA TO BEITBRIDGE

BEITBRIDGE TO HARARE

HARARE TO BEITBRIDGE

Victoria Falls to Beitbridge:

757 — VICTORIA FALLS — 0
A8
47
ZAMBIA Zambezi
ZIMBABWE
53
Matetsi
Deka
651 — Hwange — 106
50
Gwayi
Kamativi
17
Gwayi River Mine
Hwange National Park
17
567 — Gwayi River — 190
26
541 — Halfway House — 216
Tsholotsho
50
A8
Lupane
31
460 — Kenmaur — 297
Gwayi
Bubi
Sawmills
98
Lonely Mine
Nyamandhlovu
Tshotsholo
A8
42
Plumtree — A7 — 320 — BULAWAYO — 437
A5 — Gweru
A6
Matobo National Park
66
MATOBO HILLS
Thuli
Lake Cunningham
Mbalabala
60
Matobo National Park
Zvishavane
194 — Gwanda — 563
Silababuhwa Dam
Guyu
45
Zvishavane
149 — West Nicolson — 608
Umzingwane
29
Tamba
27
30
Towla
63 — Mazunga — 694
A6
63
Limpopo
A4
Masvingo
0 — BEITBRIDGE — 757
SOUTH AFRICA
ZIMBABWE

Harare to Beitbridge:

578 — HARARE — A3
A5
Chegutu
Marondera
Lake Chivero
Manyame
Marondera
A4
55
523 — Beatrice
Mubayira
Mapfure
86
Munyati
Zamatobwe
437 — Chivhu
A4
Buhera
51
386 — Mvuma
Gweru
Gutu
48
Mashava
A4
53
Shagashi
285 — A9 — Masvingo — A9 — Mutare
Mandamabwe
Lake Mutirikwe
Mushandike Dam
23
Glenlivat
Great Zimbabwe National Monument
Mandamabwe
Bangala Dam
72
A4
Ngundu — A10 — Triangle
12
Runde
43
135 — Rutenga
18
117 — Mwenezi
42
Mwenzi
Toula
A4
75 — Bubi
Bubi
75
Mazunga
A6 — A4
ZIMBABWE
Limpopo
SOUTH AFRICA
0 — BEITBRIDGE

Copyright © Map Studio

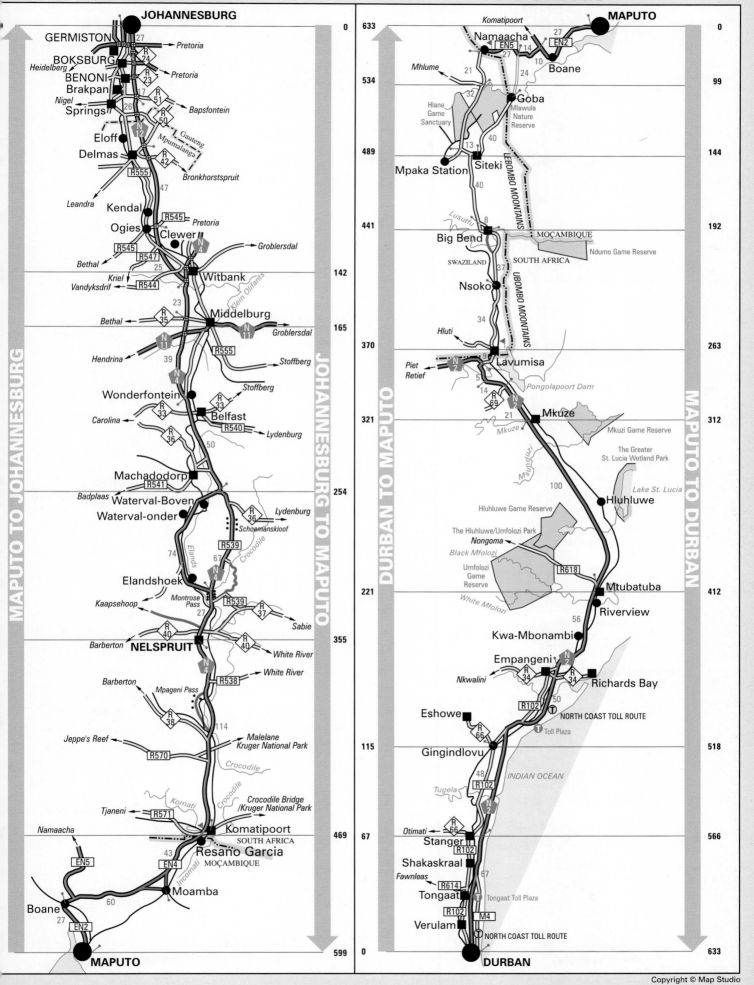

Copyright © Map Studio

BEITBRIDGE TO JOHANNESBURG

PRETORIA TO BLOEMFONTEIN

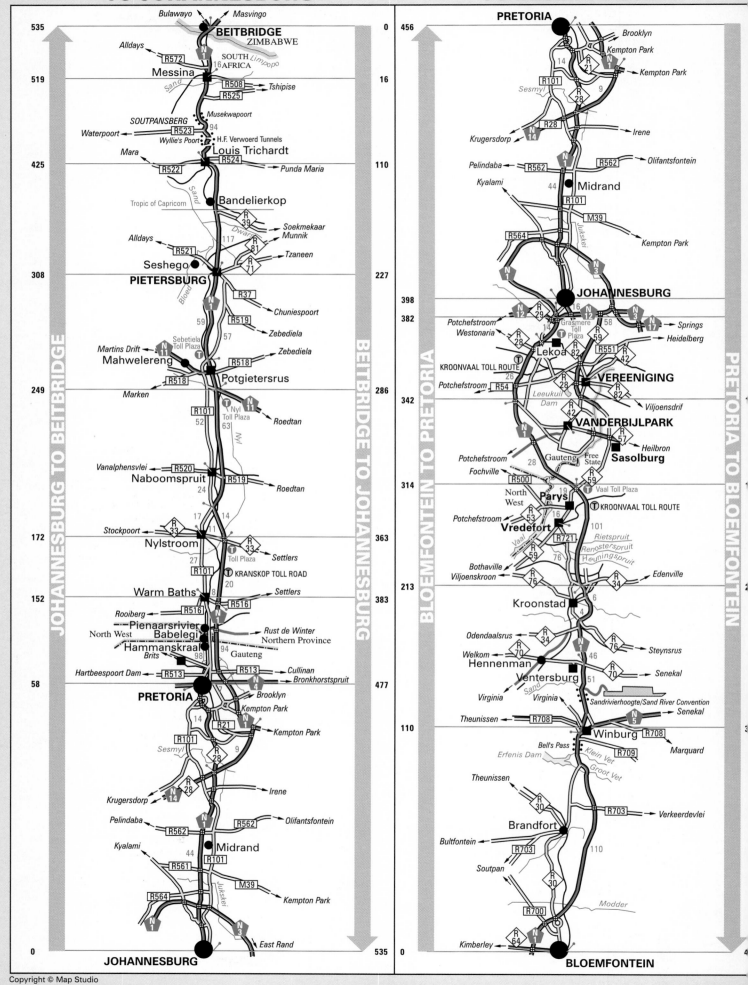

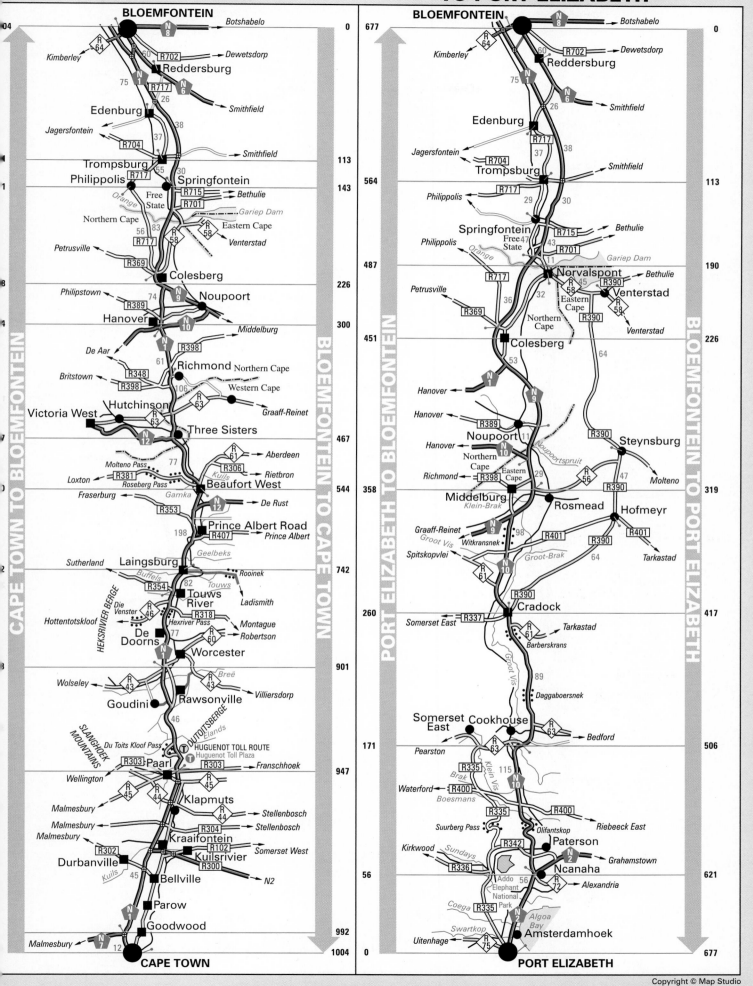

Copyright © Map Studio

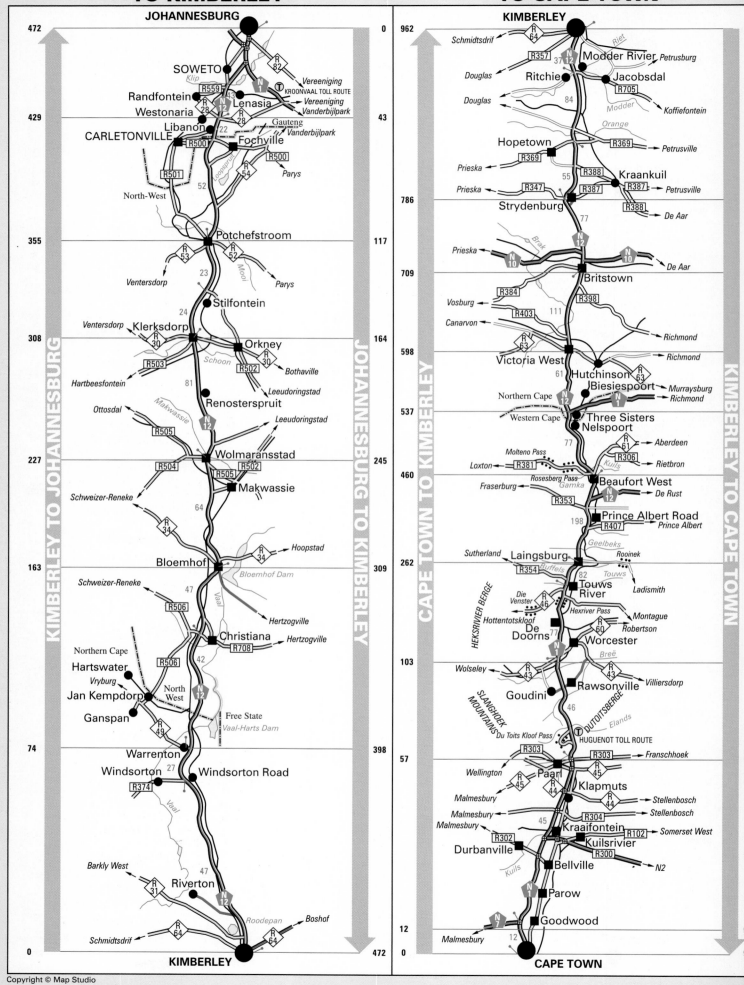

Copyright © Map Studio

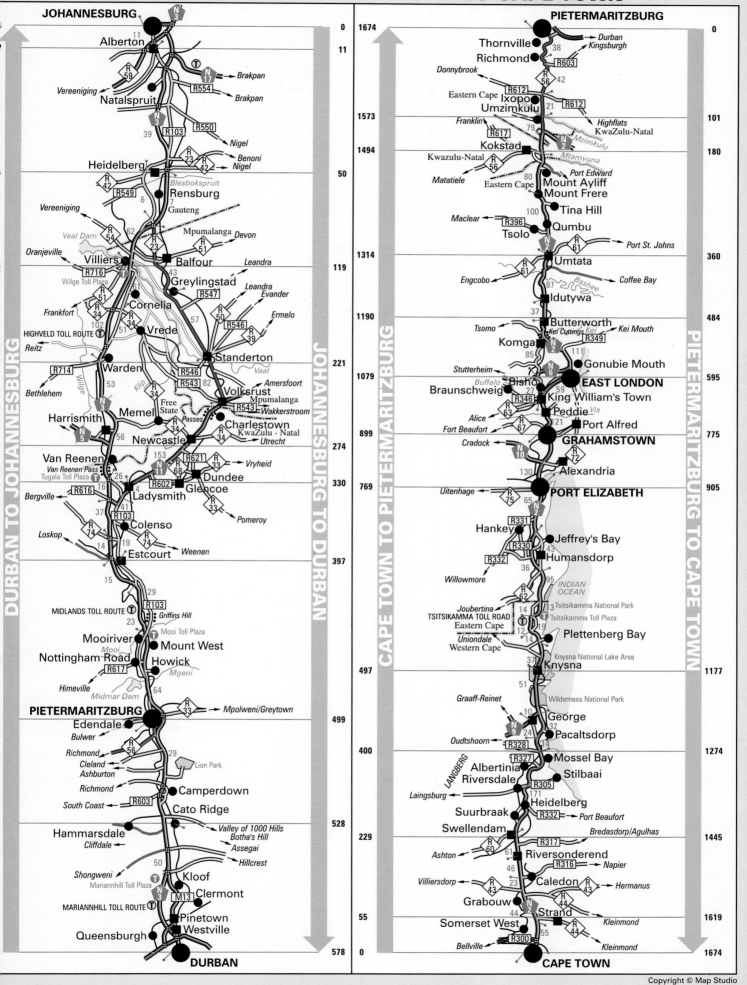

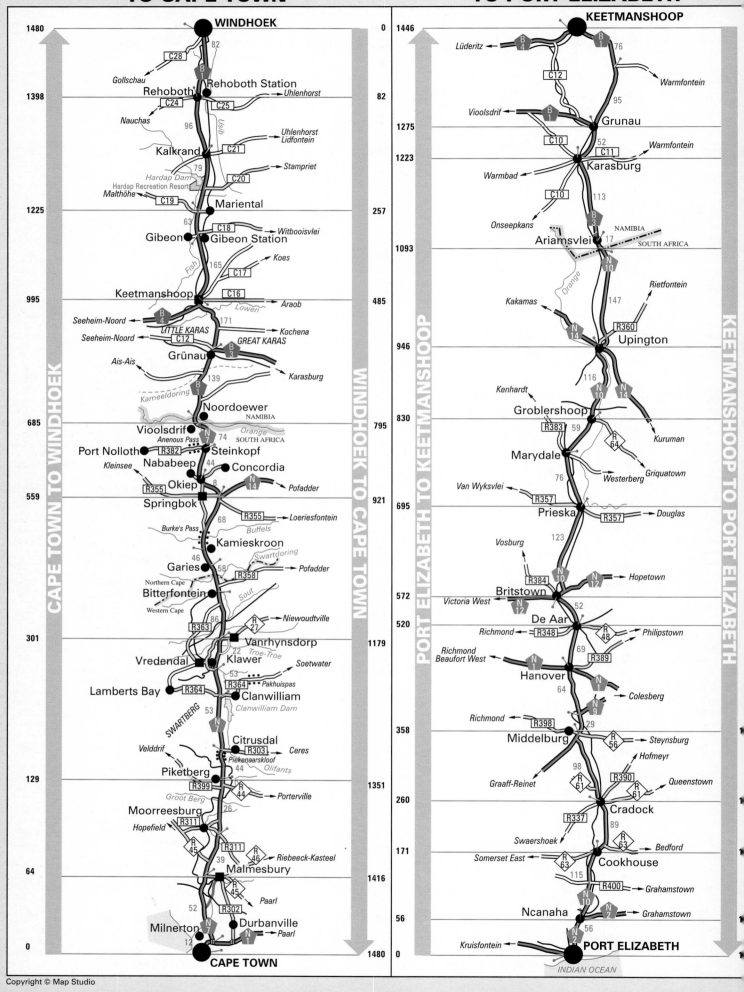

Copyright © Map Studio

INDEX TO PLACE NAMES

ABBREVIATIONS: E.C. - Eastern Cape N.P. - Northern Province N.W. - North-West F.S. - Free State
KZN - KwaZulu-Natal W.C. - Western Cape N.C. - Northern Cape Mpum. - Mpumalanga Gau. - Gauteng
RSA - South Africa Moç. - Moçambique Zim. - Zimbabwe Zam. - Zambia Nam. - Namibia Bots. - Botswana

AALWYNSFONTEIN - CHIKWAWA

INDEX TO PLACE NAMES

CHILALA - GRÜNAU

INDEX TO PLACE NAMES

GRUNDORNER - LETLHAKENG

INDEX TO PLACE NAMES

LETSHENG - MUGULAMA

INDEX TO PLACE NAMES

MUHEMBO - QOLORA MOUTH

INDEX TO PLACE NAMES

QOMBOLO - THE HAVEN

ACKNOWLEDGEMENTS

Cartography
Gary Coughlan, Annette Thomas, Barbara Brightwell,
Sarah Fulcher, Robert Gracie,
Andrew Aikman

Research
Christopher Hosken, Judy Graham

Compilation
Anthony Keeling, Broderick Kupka

Design
Karien Matthews, Annette Thomas
Mark Hedington

The publishers acknowledge with thanks the assistance, in the compilation of this Atlas, received from Government Departments, Municipal Authorities, Publicity Departments and many other bodies, both public and private.

Photographic Credits
Walter Knirr
Cape Recife Lighthouse - (page 9)
Drakensberg View (page 15)
Namaqualand Flowers (page 10)
Victoria and Alfred Waterfront (page 3)
Flowers in the Namib (page 24)
Dune at Sossusvlei (cover)

Anthony Bannister Photo Library
Aerial view of Ponto do Ouro - Stefania Lamberti (page 41)
Diver with school of fish - Peter Pinnock (page 3)
Moçambique Island - Andrew Bannister (page 53)

Anton van Zyl
Ghost mining town of Kolmanskop (page 16)

Struik Image Library
Victoria Falls - Roger de la Harpe (page 3)
Lion in the Kruger National Park (page 23) and
Mostert's Mill (page 55) - Lanz von Horston

Wild Frontiers
The Africa Travel Specialists, P.O. Box 844, Halfway House, 1685
Tel. +27 11 315-4838   Fax. +27 11 315-4850
Etosha waterhole (page 3)

1st Edition copyright Map Studio MCMXCVII. All rights reserved. No part of this publication may be reproduced, stored in a retrieval system, or transmitted in any form or by any means, electronic, electrostatic, magnetic tape, mechanical, photocopying, recording or otherwise, without the prior permission in writing of the copyright owner.

AMENDMENTS?

Do you wish to point out an error, make an amendment or suggest an improvement?
You can do this by sending us a letter from anywhere in South Africa and you don't have to pay postage.
Simply address your envelope to:-

Freepost JHZ4417
Attention: The Research Department
Map Studio
P O Box 624
BERGVLEI
2012

Or else fax your proposed changes/improvements to **(011) 444-3952**

Please include the following information:

Publication ....

Edition...

Proposed changes...
....
....
....
....
....
....
....

Name...
Postal Address...
Code..

Tel. ....
Occupation...

**YOU CAN ALSO SEND YOUR INFORMATION NOW TO
OUR E-MAIL ADDRESS.
SIMPLY ADDRESS IT TO:
RESEARCH @ MAPSTUDIO.CO.ZA**

MapStudio
A DIVISION OF THE STRUIK PUBLISHING GROUP
You'd be lost without us